You are HIS Child

Scott Hicks

Copyright © 2025 by Scott Hicks

All rights reserved.

No part of this book may be reproduced, stored in a retrieval system, or transmitted in any form or by any means—electronic, mechanical, photocopying, recording, or otherwise—without the prior written permission of the author, except for brief quotations in critical reviews or articles.

Cover design by Scott Hicks

Scripture references are taken from *The King James Version* of the Bible or *The Book of Mormon* unless otherwise noted.

This book is a work of nonfiction. Any references to real people, events, or locales are intended solely to provide context for the author's personal experiences and scriptural interpretations.

ISBN: 9798306509983

Whether you're wrestling with trauma, feeling unworthy of God's love, or just trying to hold on for another day, my hope is to remind you that you are not alone. Jesus is real, Heavenly Father is real. You are His child, and that truth can change everything. Don't ever give up! You are special. You are loved.

If you are in crisis or need immediate help, please reach out to the **National Suicide Prevention Lifeline** by dialing **988** or texting **HOME** to **741741** for free, confidential support 24/7. You are never alone, and there is always someone ready to listen.

Contents

1. Introduction: Why This Book? — 1
2. Chapter 1: You Are Not Forgotten — 7
3. Chapter 2: He Knows Your Pain — 16
4. Chapter 3: Overcoming Addiction — 26
5. Chapter 4: When Loneliness Feels Overwhelming — 35
6. Chapter 5: Understanding God's Plan for You — 44
7. Chapter 6: Finding Strength With Others — 53
8. Chapter 7: Healing the Broken Heart — 62
9. Chapter 8: Trusting God Through Hard Times — 70
10. Chapter 9: The Power of Forgiveness — 78
11. Chapter 10: Rising Above Shame — 86
12. Chapter 11: Learning to Hear His Voice — 93
13. Chapter 12: Serving Others in Love — 101
14. Chapter 13: The Atonement Is Personal — 108

15.	Chapter 14: Holding on to Hope Through Mental Health Struggles	116
16.	Chapter 15: Rediscovering Joy	122
17.	Chapter 16: Loving Yourself as God Loves You	129
18.	Chapter 17: Letting Your Light Shine	135
19.	Chapter 18: Holding On to Faith When Prayers Seem Unanswered	142
20.	Chapter 19: Looking to the Savior in Every Season	152
21.	Chapter 20: Embracing Your Divine Heritage	157
22.	Conclusion & Final Invitation	164
23.	Bibliography	169

Introduction: Why This Book?

I'm so grateful you picked up this book. If we were sitting together in a comfortable living room right now, maybe sipping cocoa, I'd want to look you in the eyes and tell you something important: You matter more than you realize. You are not alone. Life can get heavy, and I'm guessing you're feeling that weight or know someone who is. Sometimes it's a weight we can't quite describe, like loneliness or discouragement. Other times, it's big and obvious, like addiction, abuse, or overwhelming stress. Whatever it is, I want you to know right from the start that you have a Savior who loves you. You have a Heavenly Father who hasn't forgotten you. And that truth, which might feel like a small glimmer of light, is actually more powerful than all the darkness life can throw your way.

I'm not here to lecture, and I'm definitely not here to make you feel guilty or inadequate. Instead, think of me as a friend who's experienced the ups and downs of life and has discovered something so valuable that I can't help but share it. I want to talk to you about Jesus Christ and our

Heavenly Father in a way that feels personal and kind, without a bunch of fancy words. Jesus Himself was never about showy speeches; He spoke in parables and simple stories so people from every walk of life could feel His message. He told us that He came "to heal the brokenhearted" (Luke 4:18, KJV). If you're reading this because your heart feels bruised or shattered, please know you're exactly the person He was talking about.

You might wonder if that healing is meant for someone else—someone holier, someone with fewer mistakes, or someone who's never faced the same challenges as you. You might feel that Jesus is too disappointed in you and has turned away or walked on, leaving you in the mud. But those are just lies that satan always tells us. The Savior's invitation was, and is, for all. He said, "Come unto me, **all** ye that labour and are heavy laden, and I will give you rest" (Matthew 11:28, KJV). He didn't say "some of you who qualify" or "only those who haven't messed up too badly." He said all. That word is powerful. It includes everyone, regardless of what you've done or how unworthy you might feel.

I love how personal Jesus is when He interacts with people in the scriptures. He doesn't treat them like projects; He treats them like friends, or even better, like family. And you are family. You are a child of God. That might sound like a phrase we hear in Sunday School, but it's a profound reality. To be a child of God means there is something divine in your very DNA. No matter how far you've fallen or how broken you feel, there is an eternal spark within you that comes straight from the God of the universe, your Heavenly Father. Because of that spark, you are worthy of love, belonging, and healing.

I know that's sometimes hard to believe when life is pounding at your door. It's like being stuck out in a raging storm with thunder crashing so loudly you can't hear yourself think. In those moments, it's easy to forget that there's a Savior inside the house, beckoning you to come in and warm up by the fire. Maybe you feel like you don't deserve to step inside, or you're too dirty, or maybe you think the door's locked, or maybe you're too exhausted even to try the handle. But I promise you, the door is open. Jesus stands on the other side, calling your name. And once you're inside that grace and warmth, you'll wonder why you hesitated for so long.

Yes, there are a thousand reasons why you might feel distant from God right now. Maybe you've been deeply hurt by someone who claimed to represent Him. Maybe you've prayed a hundred prayers and felt no relief. Maybe you've heard conflicting voices—some telling you that God's love is conditional, or that you have to follow a strict set of rules before He'll even glance your way. Let me gently assure you: His love isn't a reward; it's freely given. Elder Jeffrey R. Holland once said that God's love "is simply always there" (Holland, 2012, p. 44). It's an unbreakable promise, woven into the very fabric of our existence.

You might be wondering, "Then why do I still feel so alone? Why do I suffer?" That's a fair question. We could spend hours discussing the nature of trials and the purpose of adversity, but let's keep it simple: Mortality involves struggle, not because Heavenly Father wants to watch us squirm, but because growth often sprouts in the soil of hardship. Jesus didn't promise a storm-free life, but He did promise He'd stand with us in every storm. In the Book of Mormon, there's a verse that says God "will console you in your afflictions" (Jacob 3:1, Book of Mormon). That's a personal, hands-on promise to comfort you right in the thick of whatever you're facing. And when God consoles, He doesn't do it with a cold pat on the back; He gathers you like a mother hen gathers her chicks (Matthew 23:37, KJV). He shelters you from the storm's worst blasts.

I get that sometimes we just want relief right now. We don't want to hear that there's "purpose" in our pain. We just want the pain gone. This book is here to validate that yearning and also to gently point you toward the arms of Jesus Christ, who understands your pain better than anyone who ever lived. The Atonement of Jesus Christ isn't just about forgiving sins; it's about Him descending below everything we could ever face (Doctrine and Covenants 88:6, The Church of Jesus Christ of Latter-day Saints, 2013). That means He felt the weight of every addiction, every fear, every heartbreak, every betrayal. Because He experienced it, He can help lift it.

If we were chatting about this in person, I would also acknowledge that faith doesn't mean ignoring professional help. Sometimes, God answers our prayers through counselors, doctors, medication, support groups, or caring friends. There is no shame in seeking help—only courage. Just as the Good Samaritan bandaged wounds and took the injured man to an inn (Luke 10:34, KJV), so too can modern resources serve as healing balm. Heavenly Father is eager to guide us toward solutions that may combine spiritual and practical approaches. Faith and science are not enemies; they are both gifts from God meant to bless our lives.

You might think, "Okay, I'm hearing you. But what's the plan here? How does this book help?" Think of each chapter as a warm conversation about topics that can be really tough: abuse, addiction, loneliness, shame, mental health struggles, and more. We'll talk about how Jesus Christ and Heavenly Father fit into each of these challenges. We'll look at what the scriptures say, but in a plain and comforting way, rather than a stern or academic way. We'll also explore quotes from people who have spent their lives trying to point us back to God. And we'll do it without diving into complicated theological debates. This is about the basics: that you are loved, that you have worth, and that through Jesus Christ, you can overcome even the darkest moments.

I hope as you read, you'll feel like we're just two friends chatting. John Bytheway, a popular author, has a gift for making spiritual principles feel personal and inviting. He strikes that note of, "Hey, let's walk together and figure this out," rather than "Here are all the ways you're doing life wrong." That's exactly what I want for us: a safe, uplifting journey where you feel encouraged to keep going. In one of his talks, Bytheway said something along the lines of, "Heavenly Father's greatest hope for you is that you come back home" (Bytheway, 2009, p. 23). That's the whole point. It's about returning to our heavenly home with more wisdom and empathy than we had before. And Jesus Christ is the bridge that makes that return possible.

When we reach the end of this book, my prayer is that you'll feel a deeper connection to your Savior and a renewed sense of hope. I'm not here to fix every problem in your life—no mortal can do that—but I do believe in a God who can bring us peace in the chaos. You don't have to carry your burdens alone anymore. Handing them over to Jesus might sound simplistic, but it's actually the most profound act of trust we can perform. If you're not sure how to do that yet, that's okay. We'll talk about it in the pages ahead. One step at a time, one prayer at a time, you can find relief.

So if you're ready, let's walk this road together. And if you're not ready—if you're just peeking into this book with one eye open, unsure if you can handle a spiritual pep talk—feel free to read a little and see if it resonates. We won't rush. The truth of your divine worth isn't going anywhere. God isn't going anywhere. He waits patiently, arms outstretched, waiting for the day you look up and realize you're not forgotten or abandoned. You are, and always have been, His beloved child.

I'm thrilled and humbled to share these messages with you. Whether you read quickly or slowly, whether you highlight half the book or just skim the pages, I hope something here will nourish your soul. If you find a sentence or two that brings light to your day, consider it a personal gift from a Father in Heaven who adores you and wants you to know it. Let that sink in: You are worth adoring. Sometimes we think that can't possibly be true, but it is. So, with a grateful heart, I welcome you to this journey. Let's discover together how deeply Jesus Christ loves us and how that love can transform our darkest nights into dawn.

Thank you for being here. Thank you for being brave enough to hope. Let's begin.

Chapter 1: You Are Not Forgotten

I want to start by talking about something that often goes unspoken: that feeling of being overlooked, invisible, or too broken for anyone to care. It's that nagging thought in the back of our minds that says, "No one really understands or likes me." If you've felt that way—maybe this very morning or maybe for years—then you're in the right place. Because if there's one thing I want you to hear loud and clear, it's this: You are not forgotten by your Heavenly Father or by Jesus Christ. They know you perfectly. They see beyond the outer layers we wear. They see your heart, including the cracks and scars, and they love you exactly as you are, while also seeing who you can become.

It might help to visualize how Jesus interacted with people in the New Testament. For instance, He never hesitated to connect with those who society deemed "less than." Think of the woman with the issue of blood who was brave enough to touch His garment in a crowded street. She'd suffered twelve long years and had spent all her money on physicians who couldn't help her (Mark 5:25-34, KJV). Yet Jesus noticed her in the midst of that throng. He didn't say, "Oh, sorry, I'm busy, please take a number." He paused everything just for her. He asked, "Who touched my clothes?" not because He didn't know, but because He wanted her to know that He saw her as a precious individual. And then, with infinite tenderness, He called her "daughter." Imagine the comfort in that single word! It affirmed she wasn't just a random face in the crowd; she was cherished family to Him.

Have you ever felt like the person stuck in the crowd, desperate for help but unsure if anyone, especially the Savior, would notice you? The story in Mark reminds us that He is both willing and eager to reach out to us personally. Our pains, no matter how chronic or complicated, matter to Him. Sometimes we might think our problems are too small or too big for God, but in my experience, there's no such thing. The same Jesus who performed miracles of physical healing can heal our hearts, calm our anxieties, and breathe peace into our struggles.

One of my favorite things about the Savior is that He looks beyond the labels we or others might stick on us. If you struggle with depression or anxiety, you may have been labeled by those conditions. Perhaps well-meaning people have tried to fix you with quick advice that doesn't really help, making you feel even more invisible. But Jesus sees more than a label or a diagnosis. He sees the entirety of who you are—a beloved soul with hopes, fears, talents, and dreams. And when He looks at you, His heart is filled with compassion, not frustration.

Elder Dieter F. Uchtdorf taught that "though we are incomplete, God loves us completely" (Uchtdorf, 2009, p. 75). That's incredibly comforting. Even when we haven't figured ourselves out, even when we're at our most insecure, God's love isn't wavering. It's kind of like that unwavering love a good parent feels for a child—only infinitely more. Even if that child draws on the walls with permanent marker, knocks over a priceless vase, or comes home past curfew, the love is still there. Yes, there might be consequences and lessons, but true parental love remains. Multiply that feeling by a million, and you have Heavenly Father's love for you.

Maybe you're thinking, "Okay, that's a nice idea. But I still feel alone." I hear you. Feeling alone can persist even when we intellectually know God loves us. Sometimes our emotions take a while to catch up with our spiritual understanding. That's okay. Feelings can be tricky. But as we nurture our relationship with Heavenly Father—through prayer, scripture study, or simply by talking openly with Him about our day—those feelings can gradually shift. It's not always an instant transformation, but a slow, steady process where God's love seeps into the cracks of our hearts, bit by bit, until one day we realize we aren't so lonely anymore.

Let's talk about practical ways to open ourselves to that divine love. One way is to pray with absolute honesty. I used to think prayer had to be formal, with certain phrases in a certain order. But the more I see prayer as a conversation with the most loving Father imaginable, the more real it becomes. Sometimes we just need to say, "Heavenly Father, this is tough. I'm scared, and I don't know what to do. Please help me. Help me feel Your love." That kind of heartfelt prayer, even if it's clumsy, can be a powerful step toward feeling that reassuring sense that we're not alone in the universe. If words fail you, you can even pour out your heart silently, because God knows the unspoken language of our souls.

Another way to feel God's love is by reading scripture in a personal way. Instead of seeing the scriptures as ancient texts, try viewing them as love letters or personal messages. For example, when you come across a verse that says "I have loved thee with an everlasting love" (Jeremiah 31:3, KJV), pause and whisper it to yourself like God is saying it to you, personally: "I have loved you, [your name], with an everlasting love." Let the words settle in. If you also read the Book of Mormon, find passages there that echo this message, like "Ye are free; ye are permitted to act for yourselves" (Helaman 14:30, Book of Mormon). That's God telling us He trusts us to make choices, that we're not just puppets. It's a sign of deep respect and love.

And it's totally okay if you feel like you don't have the energy for scripture study every day. Sometimes the best we can do is read a single verse or even just remember one from memory. God isn't a cosmic professor waiting to fail us for not doing all the assigned reading. He's a loving Father who rejoices in any effort we make to connect with Him. If all you have in you is to sit quietly and think, "I believe You're there, God. I believe You love me," that can be enough for that moment.

Now, I want to address something crucial: sometimes, despite our best efforts, we still feel weighed down by circumstances outside our control. It could be an abusive relationship, a toxic work environment, or a personal crisis that just won't quit. In those cases, remember Jesus understands suffering on a level we can't fully comprehend. Elder Neal A. Maxwell once said that part of the majesty of the Atonement is that Jesus can empathize perfectly with every pain we experience, no matter how unique (Maxwell, 1985, p. 18). That empathy isn't just a warm sentiment; it's a tangible power that can strengthen us to do hard things. If you need to set boundaries with someone who's harming you, or if you need to reach out for professional help, God's power can help you take that step. He often works through other people, like therapists, friends, or mentors. Don't be afraid to use those lifelines. Reaching out isn't a sign of weak faith; it's often a sign of trusting God enough to accept the rescue He's sending through His earthly helpers.

Let's get personal for a moment. There was a time in my life when I felt completely disconnected from God. It was a tough season—problems with my health, my finances, and my relationships all seemed to hit at once. People would say, "Just pray more," or "Read the scriptures, you'll be fine," but it felt like none of that was making a difference. My prayers felt like they were bouncing off the ceiling. I wondered if God was ignoring me or if I'd simply used up my quota of divine help. But during that dark time, I had a small moment of clarity while reading the New Testament. I came across the verse where Jesus says, "I will not leave you comfortless: I will come to you" (John 14:18, KJV). As I read it, I felt a whisper of hope, a warm presence in my heart that I couldn't deny. It wasn't an instant fix for all my problems, but it was enough to remind me that God was aware of me. Over the next few months, small miracles and acts of kindness from other people kept pointing me back to that promise. Bit by bit, the clouds began to lift.

I share that because sometimes we think we need a massive, cinematic miracle to confirm God's love. But in reality, God often works in gentle, steady ways. He might send a timely text from a friend, a hymn that pops into your mind unexpectedly, or a random compliment from a coworker that gives you a boost. These aren't coincidences; they're love notes from a God who is intricately involved in our lives. The trick is to notice them. If we're convinced that God doesn't love us, we might brush off these moments as pure chance. But if we open our eyes and our hearts, we'll see that He's been orchestrating tender mercies all along.

What if you say, "I've never felt that. I don't get those tender mercies"? That's a tough place to be. But please don't assume that because you haven't recognized them yet, they don't exist. Sometimes life's noises are so loud that we can't hear the whisper. Or perhaps we're expecting a certain kind of miracle (like a specific outcome to a prayer), and when it doesn't happen, we think God hasn't answered. But He might be answering in a different way. Elder David A. Bednar described how answers can come like a sunrise (gradual and subtle) rather than a light switch (instant and bright) (Bednar, 2011, p. 49). If you haven't recognized a sunrise answer yet, keep looking. It might be dawning slowly around you.

Another piece of this puzzle is learning to see yourself as worth loving. God's love is unconditional, but sometimes we build our own walls of self-doubt. We think, "He can't possibly love me. I've done too many bad things." Or "I'm not special enough. I haven't served a mission, or I barely go to church, or I don't even know if I believe." But Jesus embraced people from all walks of life, including sinners, skeptics, and outcasts. The only people He really got stern with were the self-righteous who acted like they didn't need Him. If you feel broken, you're exactly who He came to lift. Feeling unworthy actually puts you in a perfect position to realize just how big His grace is. He said, "They that be whole need not a physician, but they that are sick" (Matthew 9:12, KJV). If you're spiritually or emotionally "sick," guess what? He's ready to be your physician, no strings attached.

Martin Luther King Jr. once stated, "Darkness cannot drive out darkness; only light can do that" (King, 1963, p. 45). That resonates with me because Jesus Christ is the ultimate Light (John 8:12, KJV). When we invite Him into our personal darkness, He doesn't show up with condemnation; He shows up with illumination. Darkness flees in the presence of His love. Over time, the more we let Him in, the more that darkness loses its grip. Does it vanish overnight? Not usually, but light is persistent. Even a small candle in a large room changes the entire atmosphere. Jesus can be that candle, gently pushing back the shadows and offering warmth where we feel numb.

Maybe you worry that inviting Jesus in means changing your life in ways you're not ready for. That's understandable. Change can be scary. But remember, He's a patient tutor. He'll walk with you step by step, never forcing or rushing you. As you get to know Him, your heart will naturally start shifting. You'll find yourself wanting to be more kind, more forgiving, more open to goodness. It's less about a rigid checklist and more about a transformation from the inside out. And the best part is, He'll love you at every stage of that transformation. You don't have to wait until you're "fixed" to approach Him. Approach Him broken, and let Him help piece you back together.

I also want to emphasize that if you're struggling with severe mental health issues, don't hesitate to seek professional help. Prayer and scripture study are vital, but they're not meant to replace therapy or medication when those are needed. They can work together beautifully. Heavenly Father is not disappointed in us if we use all available tools to heal. Think of it this way: If you broke your leg, you'd pray, but you'd also see a doctor and probably use crutches for a while. The same principle applies to our minds and hearts. It's okay—no, it's good—to get help.

Let me share something I find comforting: Pope Francis once said, "God never tires of forgiving us; we are the ones who tire of seeking his mercy" (Francis, 2013, p. 8). That reminds me that if I'm feeling distant, maybe I'm the one who's holding back. God's arms are still wide open, eager to embrace me. So, if you've pulled away because of shame or frustration, consider that maybe He's still right there, waiting, ready to shower you with the love you've been missing.

Finally, I want you to know that this first chapter is just the beginning of a journey we'll take together in this book. We'll delve into specific struggles—like abuse, addiction, loneliness, and more—and see how Jesus fits into all of them. He's not a one-size-fits-all remedy; rather, He's a deeply personal Savior who meets each of us in the exact way we need. It might be a slow process, but it's a real one.

Here's a challenge for you. If you're up for it, sometime this week, find a quiet moment. Maybe it's after everyone's gone to bed, or maybe it's while you're walking outside. Close your eyes (unless you're walking in traffic—then maybe just keep them open!) and say, "Jesus, if You're there, help me feel a little bit of Your love. Help me know that I'm not forgotten." Then notice what happens in the days that follow. Maybe you'll feel a subtle warmth in your heart, maybe a friend will reach out unexpectedly, or maybe a verse in the scriptures will stand out to you in a new way. Those little signals can be sweet reminders that yes, He is there, and yes, He sees you.

As we move forward, please keep in mind that your worth is not up for debate. Heavenly Father established it the moment He created your soul. No mistake you've made, no wound you've received, and no label the world slaps on you can lessen that worth. You are infinitely, eternally, and unshakably loved. Jesus Christ's willingness to suffer for each one of us (Alma 7:11, Book of Mormon) is a testament to how precious we are in His eyes.

I hope you feel a little lighter, a little more hopeful after reading this. And if you don't yet, that's okay—keep going. Sometimes the dawn breaks slowly. Just remember that a single ray of light can shatter the darkness, and that light is waiting for you in the loving arms of your Savior, Jesus Christ. He's been waiting all along, whispering your name, hoping you'll discover (or rediscover) what it means to be cherished by a Father in Heaven who created you for greater things than you can possibly imagine.

In the next chapters, we'll talk about real struggles—things that might be weighing you down right now. But every step of the way, we'll bring it back to Jesus and the truth that He offers not a lecture, but a lifeline. You don't have to tackle the future all at once; just walk with Him today. One day at a time, one prayer at a time, that's how lives change. That's how hope is reborn. And that's how we begin to see, with greater and greater clarity, that indeed—we are His children. And in that identity lies more hope and power than you might have ever dreamed.

Chapter 2: He Knows Your Pain

Sometimes when we hear the word "abuse," our minds go straight to dramatic news headlines or stories we wish only existed in fiction. But the reality of abuse can be far more personal and, sadly, closer to home than many of us realize. Abuse can be physical, emotional, verbal, or even spiritual—and it often leaves deep scars that aren't visible on the surface. If you're reading this and have experienced any kind of abuse, my heart aches for you. It's a very real and heavy cross to bear. You might wonder where Jesus Christ and Heavenly Father are in all of this. How could a loving God allow such pain? My hope in this chapter is to gently remind you that although people can be cruel and life can be unfair, neither Jesus nor our Heavenly Father has abandoned you. If anything, They are reaching out more earnestly to you, hoping you'll discover that Their love is steady and healing in a world that sometimes feels so harsh.

One of the most beautiful truths I've learned is that God doesn't shame us for being victims. He doesn't blame us or ask what we did to deserve this.

Our Savior weeps with those who weep (John 11:35, King James Version). He mourns with those who mourn (Mosiah 18:9, Book of Mormon). And yes, He rages against injustice. In the scriptures, we see Jesus flipping tables in the temple when He witnessed the sacredness of His Father's house being defiled (Matthew 21:12, KJV). This same protective Savior is equally passionate about the sanctity of our bodies, hearts, and spirits. If He could show such righteous indignation over money changers in the temple, imagine how He feels when someone hurts His precious children.

But when you're the one who's been hurt, you might feel confusion, shame, or an overwhelming sense of powerlessness. You might even question your own worth. Abuse has a twisted way of making us doubt that we deserve love, or worse, making us believe we're somehow responsible for what happened. Let me say something clearly, as if I were sitting right next to you and looking you straight in the eyes: You are not to blame for someone else's choice to harm you. Period. Abuse is never okay. You are a child of God, and He condemns the acts of those who violate the sacred gift of agency by harming others. Billy Graham once said, "God never intended for us to live in bondage to fear" (Graham, 1984, p. 27). Yet abuse can lock us in just that—fear. It's real, but it doesn't define who you are. God sees you as infinitely more than the harm done to you.

It's also important to recognize that healing from abuse often requires more than just prayer—though prayer is a powerful tool. Sometimes, we need professionals who understand trauma, or trusted friends and family, or support groups where we can share our burdens. If you feel prompted to seek help, that's not a lack of faith; it's an act of courage. The Good Samaritan in the Bible didn't just say a prayer over the wounded traveler and keep walking; he took the man to an inn and made sure he got proper care (Luke 10:34, KJV). Heavenly Father frequently answers prayers through earthly angels: counselors, doctors, and empathetic friends who can walk with us through our pain.

You might wonder where God is while this abuse is going on or has gone on. That's a tender question, one that can tug at our hearts. We don't always get neat, tidy answers to "Why?" Elder Jeffrey R. Holland taught that we sometimes face trials without fully understanding them in mortality, but we can trust in a God whose love surpasses our pain (Holland, 2012, p. 31). There is a scripture in the Book of Mormon that says God "will console you in your afflictions" (Jacob 3:1, Book of Mormon). That word "console" paints an image of a loving Father who wraps us in His arms when we're hurting. Even if the abuse happened behind closed doors and no one else knows, God knows. He sees every tear. And more importantly, He validates your pain.

Validation is something many abuse survivors don't receive from those around them. Sometimes, people around us might say, "Oh, it wasn't that bad," or "Are you sure you're not exaggerating?" or "Just forgive and forget." While forgiveness is indeed a powerful principle, it doesn't mean pretending the abuse never happened or that the pain was insignificant. Real forgiveness, in a gospel sense, involves acknowledging the wrongdoing, setting healthy boundaries, and entrusting ultimate justice to God. Abuse isn't just a small misstep; it's a grievous violation of one's personal dignity. Our Savior, who was Himself mocked, tortured, and ultimately crucified, deeply understands what it feels like to be on the receiving end of brutality. When Isaiah says the Messiah was "despised and rejected of men; a man of sorrows, and acquainted with grief" (Isaiah 53:3, KJV), he wasn't kidding. Jesus truly knows.

In knowing that Jesus fully comprehends our trauma, we discover a new kind of hope. We realize we don't cry alone. We can approach Him in prayer, honestly stating our fears, anger, and even our confusion over where He was during our darkest hours. Sometimes, sharing those raw emotions with God is the first step toward healing. It's like taking a thorn out of a festering wound; it hurts to address it, but ignoring it usually leads to more pain in the long run. Elder Dieter F. Uchtdorf once suggested that Heavenly Father is "not waiting to love you until you have overcome your weaknesses and bad habits. He loves you today" (Uchtdorf, 2009, p. 70). If that's true for our sins and mistakes, it's certainly true for our suffering. We don't have to wait until we're "fully healed" to go to Him. He wants to walk with us in our healing journey.

Now, let's talk about boundaries, because they matter—especially in situations involving abuse. Some people mistakenly think that being a Christian means being perpetually passive, letting others walk all over you, or returning to an abusive situation "in the name of forgiveness." But Jesus also said we should be "wise as serpents, and harmless as doves" (Matthew 10:16, KJV). Being wise sometimes means removing ourselves from harm's way or seeking help from law enforcement or trusted clergy if necessary. Your safety—physical, emotional, and spiritual—matters deeply to your Heavenly Father. Setting a boundary is not un-Christlike; it can be a necessary step to prevent further harm and begin real healing.

One scripture that has always touched my heart is Psalm 34:18, which promises that "the Lord is nigh unto them that are of a broken heart; and saveth such as be of a contrite spirit" (KJV). If abuse has left your heart feeling shattered, you're exactly the kind of person this verse is speaking to. God draws near to the brokenhearted. That phrase itself suggests that He moves closer, not further away, when we are in the depths of sorrow. And when He moves closer, He brings with Him comfort, understanding, and, over time, the capacity to feel peace again. Peace may seem impossible right now, but with God's love, impossible things can begin to unfold.

It can also help to remember that Jesus's atoning sacrifice wasn't just about sins—it was about pains and sorrows too. Alma 7:11–12 (Book of Mormon) explains that He took upon Himself every kind of suffering, so that He might "know according to the flesh how to succor his people." That means He "gets it" intimately. He doesn't stand at a distance, offering hollow platitudes. He's been in the trenches of human agony, and that's why He's supremely qualified to heal us from wounds we ourselves can't reach.

Some survivors of abuse may wrestle with anger toward God: "Why didn't He stop it?" That's a valid question, and I won't pretend to have a perfect answer. What I do know is that we have a Heavenly Father who treasures agency, and sometimes that means people use their free will to do despicable things. It's not that God condones it. In fact, He weeps over it. But He will not infringe upon agency, because that's a core principle of His plan of salvation. Still, He promises He will restore what has been lost or broken. The Prophet Joseph Smith once taught that everything the faithful lose here on earth will be returned in the eternities, "multiplied manifold" (Smith, 1842, p. 147). While that might not erase the sting right now, it provides a glimmer of hope that justice and healing are on the horizon, if not immediately in our present. The key is holding on to the belief that God is both perfectly just and perfectly merciful, and He will set all things right in His due time.

For those who may not have personally experienced abuse but are reading to better understand or help a loved one, let me share something important: the greatest gift you can offer someone who's been hurt is to listen with compassion. Don't try to fix or judge. Don't offer quick clichés like "It was God's will" or "Time heals all wounds." Instead, remind them they are loved, that you believe them, and that their story matters. Encourage them to seek professional help if needed, and gently point them toward the Savior if they feel comfortable exploring that path. Mother Teresa said, "Being unwanted, unloved, uncared for, forgotten by everybody—I think that is a much greater hunger, a much greater poverty than the person who has nothing to eat" (Mother Teresa, 1995, p. 72). People recovering from abuse often feel that deeper kind of hunger—the hunger for acknowledgment and real support. We can be instruments in God's hands to help satisfy that hunger.

If you are the one who's been abused, please remember that God's timing and your healing process might look different from someone else's. Healing rarely follows a straight line. Some days you might feel strong, other days you might feel you've regressed. That's normal. It doesn't mean God has abandoned you, nor does it mean you aren't making progress. Each step toward acknowledging your pain, each moment of self-care, each prayer uttered—these are milestones along the path to wholeness. And wholeness is something God can restore, piece by piece, as we let Him into our story.

Another hopeful truth is that your identity is so much richer than what happened to you. Abuse can feel like it defines us, but it does not. You're defined by something much deeper: your divine nature as a child of God. Elder Russell M. Nelson (before he became President Nelson) taught that our spiritual identity is fundamental; we are "sons and daughters of an exalted God" (Nelson, 1998, p. 32). That doesn't mean the abuse is irrelevant; it means it's not the sum total of who you are. You are infinitely more than your worst experiences. The more we internalize that eternal perspective, the more we can begin to see ourselves through God's eyes—as beings of infinite worth, destined for eternal joy.

Sometimes, people might ask, "How can I use my faith to heal without feeling like I have to brush everything under the rug?" Brushing it under the rug is never what God asks us to do. Jesus was remarkably open about confronting sin and pain head-on, but always with compassion for the sinner and mercy for the wounded. If confronting the pain means seeking legal help or confiding in a church leader who can offer resources, then do so. If you are an abuser reading this, I plead with you: seek help, repent, and stop the cycle of harm. Our Savior died for all of us, and no one is beyond the reach of His atonement. But that atonement also demands we do our part to right our wrongs and protect others from further harm.

One question that might arise is how to let Jesus Christ's love sink deep enough to dispel the doubts and lies that abuse can plant in our minds. It starts with small moments—sincere prayer, reading a verse of scripture that speaks to your pain, listening to uplifting music that reminds you of God's love, or surrounding yourself with people who treat you kindly and respect your boundaries. Over time, these small acts create a soft place in your heart where God can plant seeds of healing. The apostle Paul taught that we are "the temple of the living God" (2 Corinthians 6:16, KJV). If we see ourselves as temples, we realize that we're sacred. And though an earthly temple can be desecrated, it can also be cleansed, rebuilt, and restored to its full glory.

I am reminded of something John Bytheway once said, that "life's too short to nurse grudges, take offense, or take any day for granted" (Bytheway, 2009, p. 44). While he wasn't specifically talking about abuse, I think the spirit of not letting bitterness consume us can still apply. Holding on to bitterness is understandable, but it can rob us of the joy the Savior wants us to feel. This doesn't mean you skip straight to "all is forgiven and forgotten." It means we let the healing and forgiveness process begin in a way that frees us from carrying the abuser's wrongdoing as an eternal burden. We place that burden at the feet of the One who said, "Come unto me, all ye that labour and are heavy laden" (Matthew 11:28, KJV). He knows exactly how to handle it.

Sometimes, you'll feel the Spirit whispering that you're more loved than you can imagine. Other times, you may feel nothing at all and wonder if God's gone silent. Know that silence in suffering is not the same as absence. Like the story of a teacher who stays quiet during the test, God's quietness often invites us to exercise faith. Even then, He's never truly distant. Hold on. Keep talking to Him even if you're only able to muster a brief cry for help. Elder David A. Bednar taught that answers to prayers sometimes come like a sunrise, gradually illuminating our minds and hearts (Bednar, 2011, p. 49). If your heart is still dark, wait for the first rays of that sunrise. They will come.

Let me also encourage you to consider the small daily habits that build spiritual resilience. Even if you can't commit to reading an entire chapter of scripture, read a verse or two. Jot down in a journal one reason you believe God cares about you, even if you're not fully convinced. Sing or hum a hymn or spiritual song that lifts your spirit. These baby steps may not feel earth-shattering, but they create an environment where healing can flourish. Just as a gardener tends to soil before planting seeds, we also prepare our hearts for God's healing by cultivating consistent, gentle spiritual habits.

Abuse can lead to isolation, where we feel no one can understand our pain. While it's true that no one can fully experience our exact anguish, there are people out there—trained counselors, fellow survivors, empathetic friends—who can listen and offer meaningful support. And above all, Jesus Christ absolutely understands. He bore every sorrow. In a very real sense, on the cross and in Gethsemane, He carried the emotional anguish of abuse victims everywhere (Mosiah 14:4–5, Book of Mormon). That is incredibly personal. It means when you kneel and pray, "Lord, I hurt," He can say, "I know exactly how that feels, and I love you fiercely."

My prayer is that as you read these words, you'll sense even the smallest glimmer of hope returning to your heart. You are not too damaged to be loved, not too broken to be healed, and not too far gone to be rescued. The Savior's arm is "lengthened out all the day long" (2 Nephi 28:32, Book of Mormon), and it's never withdrawn. When abuse makes us feel worthless, He speaks the truth about our eternal worth. When we feel too stained or helpless to approach Him, He comes searching for us, like a shepherd looking for a lost sheep (Luke 15:4, KJV). Let that image fill you with comfort. You are the one He's willing to go out into the wilderness to find.

Healing might be a process that takes time and patience, but every step toward wholeness is worth it. In the meantime, remember that your feelings of anger, sadness, and even confusion don't disqualify you from God's love. It's okay to be angry about what happened. It's okay to grieve. Don't rush yourself or anyone else to "get over it" before you're ready. Just keep moving, day by day, toward the light of Jesus Christ. One day, you'll be amazed at how far you've come and how truly free you can feel. That freedom is a gift God wants for all His children. You deserve that gift, and so does everyone who's ever felt crushed by abuse.

You may not believe it right now, but there will come a morning—whether in this life or the next—when the bitterness, shame, and horror of abuse will be swallowed up in the healing, redeeming power of Jesus Christ. And though none of us can fully erase the past, we can find peace that moves us beyond it. The Good Shepherd is waiting, ready to gather you close, speak truth into your wounded heart, and remind you that you matter. If you remember nothing else from this chapter, I hope you'll remember this: You are cherished by a God who sees every tear and every bruise, and who tenderly promises, "I will heal them" (3 Nephi 17:7, Book of Mormon). That's a promise you can cling to—and trust that He means it.

Chapter 3: Overcoming Addiction

Addiction can feel like a ravenous beast, stalking us when we're at our weakest. Whether it's a chemical dependency, like drugs or alcohol, or a behavioral trap, like pornography or gambling, addiction often leaves us feeling powerless and ashamed. We might promise ourselves—or even promise God—time and time again that we'll quit, only to relapse in a moment of weakness or stress. It's a cycle that can devastate our sense of self-worth. But here's the truth I hope you'll take away from this chapter: Jesus Christ and our Heavenly Father love you, even in the deepest pits of addiction. They know the painful knots you're tangled in, and They stand ready with a lifeline of grace, compassion, and genuine power to help you break free.

One of the hardest parts about addiction is the isolation it creates. We might avoid family, friends, and church because we're embarrassed or fear judgment. We might think, "If anyone really knew my struggle, they'd never look at me the same way again." That's the adversary's favorite lie—that we're alone and unworthy. But the Savior's message cuts through that lie with gentle clarity: "Come unto me, all ye that labour and are heavy laden, and I will give you rest" (Matthew 11:28, KJV). That doesn't say "except for addicts" or "unless you really messed up." It says all. If you're burdened by addiction, you fit perfectly into that "all."

Sometimes we think about the Atonement of Jesus Christ primarily as a solution for sin. And it is, absolutely. But it's also a solution for weakness, heartache, and every kind of mortal struggle. That includes the chains of addiction. Alma 7:11 (Book of Mormon) teaches that Jesus took upon Himself not just sins, but also pains and afflictions of every kind. Addiction certainly qualifies as a relentless affliction. The reason this matters is simple: if Christ carried it, He can help us carry it. If He overcame the grave, He can help us overcome the habits and cravings that seem larger than life.

Of course, that doesn't mean the road out of addiction is an instant miracle. Sometimes it is—but more often, it's a day-by-day, sometimes hour-by-hour battle. It might involve professional help, support groups, and accountability measures. There's no shame in needing medication, therapy, or a 12-step program. Just as the Good Samaritan used oil and wine to care for the wounded man's injuries (Luke 10:34, KJV), the Lord can use modern resources to help heal our hearts and bodies. Elder M. Russell Ballard taught that "addiction surrenders later freedom to choose," but that "recovery is possible" through the combination of Christ's atoning power and professional support (Ballard, 2010, p. 110). So, if you've felt hopeless, please let that truth sink in: recovery is not just possible, it is deeply aligned with God's desire for you.

Shame is a constant companion to addiction, convincing us we're beyond redemption. We might assume Heavenly Father's just waiting to condemn us, as though He's been keeping a tally of our relapses. But the scriptures paint a different picture. When the prodigal son returned home after wasting his inheritance, his father ran to meet him, embraced him, and threw a celebration in his honor (Luke 15:20–24, KJV). This story reminds us that our Heavenly Father is eager to welcome us back, not scold us for being gone so long. He knows the difference between our identity and our mistakes. Our identity is that of His precious child, no matter how entangled we've become in destructive habits.

If you're in the midst of addiction, you might struggle to feel the Spirit, or you might feel unworthy to pray. But that's exactly when you need prayer the most. Even a one-sentence plea—"Heavenly Father, help me hold on for one more day"—can open a door for divine assistance. If you can't bring yourself to pray out loud, pray silently. If even that feels too big a leap, ask a trusted friend to pray for you. The point is that God is not so distant or so offended by your addiction that He won't rush in with help the moment you invite Him. Pope Francis reminded us that "God never tires of forgiving us; we are the ones who tire of seeking His mercy" (Francis, 2013, p. 8). Don't be afraid to keep seeking. Don't be afraid to ask for mercy yet again. The well of Christ's love does not run dry.

It might help to take a practical approach, combining spiritual habits with tangible resources. For instance, many 12-step programs have a very Christ-centered approach that recognizes we need a power greater than ourselves to escape the cycle of addiction. There's humility in admitting we can't do this alone. That humility isn't weakness; it's wisdom. We're never meant to conquer life's hardest trials by sheer willpower. Even Jesus leaned on His Father in Gethsemane, pleading, "If thou be willing, remove this cup from me" (Luke 22:42, KJV). If the Son of God sought help from the Father in His agony, how much more do we need the Father's help in ours?

Sometimes, the shame from addiction leads to secrecy. We hide from church, from family, even from ourselves. But secrecy keeps us stuck. Confession in a safe environment—whether to a bishop, pastor, counselor, or trusted friend—can be the first step toward real change. James 5:16 (KJV) teaches us to "confess [our] faults one to another, and pray one for another, that [we] may be healed." There's a reason confession is mentioned in the context of healing. Keeping our struggles in the dark allows them to grow. Shining a light on them, in a context of love and support, is how we begin to weaken their hold.

Another critical component of overcoming addiction is forgiveness—both seeking forgiveness from God and extending forgiveness to ourselves. You might say, "But I don't deserve it. I've broken promises, hurt people around me, lied to those I love, and ruined my own life." While those consequences can be painful, the Atonement of Jesus Christ is expansive enough to cover them. Elder Holland once said that "however late you think you are, however many chances you think you have missed, however many mistakes you feel you have made... you have not traveled beyond the reach of divine love" (Holland, 2012, p. 31). We might have to deal with the aftermath of our choices, and that can be a painful journey, but in terms of being welcomed back into the arms of the Savior, there's no expiration date and no limit.

Forgiving ourselves can sometimes be the harder part. It's easy to cling to guilt, as if punishing ourselves will somehow atone for what we did. But that's not our job. Jesus already performed the Atonement. He's not asking us to replicate it; He's asking us to accept it. Of course, we strive to make amends where possible, repair relationships, and commit to living differently. But that's done in partnership with God's grace, not as a replacement for it. True repentance is about turning our hearts toward Christ, not wallowing in self-loathing.

There's also an aspect of addiction recovery that involves practical boundaries—changing our environment to reduce temptations, surrounding ourselves with people who support our new direction, and maybe even distancing ourselves from unhealthy influences. Remember, Jesus taught, "If thy right hand offend thee, cut it off" (Matthew 5:30, KJV). He wasn't advocating self-harm; He was emphasizing that we sometimes need drastic measures to remove harmful elements from our lives. If that means installing filters on your devices, avoiding certain places, or finding a new friend group, it's worth it. Every sacrifice pales in comparison to the freedom and peace we gain when we align ourselves with God.

In dealing with addiction, it's vital to address the emotional and spiritual roots. Many of us turn to addictive behaviors to self-medicate deeper pains—loneliness, anxiety, past traumas. That's where Christ's healing power can reach deeper than any quick fix. He can help us face the real issues behind the addiction. Sometimes we need professional therapy to navigate those deeper pains, and that's okay. It doesn't mean we lack faith; it means we're using every tool God has placed at our disposal. The Savior who healed the blind and raised the dead can also heal our hearts, but He may direct us to skilled, empathetic individuals who can facilitate that healing process.

If you're supporting someone with an addiction, please remember that love and healthy boundaries are not mutually exclusive. You can be compassionate without enabling. Encouraging them to seek help is an act of love, even if it feels uncomfortable. We can't force anyone to change, but we can offer the consistent reminder that they're valued and that help is available. We can also offer prayer and empathy, recognizing that addiction is a prison, not a conscious choice someone glories in. Elder Boyd K. Packer once said, "The study of the doctrines of the gospel will improve behavior quicker than the study of behavior will improve behavior" (Packer, 1977, p. 25). That doesn't mean we ignore professional help, but it does mean that as someone saturates themselves in the words of Christ, their desires can gradually shift. Light and truth have a transformative effect on the human soul.

Progress might feel excruciatingly slow, and relapses might happen. When they do, the adversary will try to tell you it's pointless. But it's not. Each time you sincerely repent and turn back to the Savior, you're learning something, strengthening a spiritual muscle. President Russell M. Nelson taught that repentance is "not an event; it is a process" (Nelson, 2019, p. 88). That process can be messy, but it's also a sign of spiritual life. The only true failure is giving up. As long as you keep trying, keep reaching out to Christ, and keep seeking the support you need, you're on the path to ultimate victory, even if it doesn't look that way from day to day.

Consider the story of the woman taken in adultery (John 8:3–11, KJV). She was publicly shamed, cornered by accusers, and by the law of Moses, she could have been stoned. Yet Jesus turned that moment into one of profound grace. He asked the accusers to look at their own sins. Then, when they left, He turned to the woman and said, "Neither do I condemn thee: go, and sin no more." He didn't excuse her behavior, but He also didn't crush her with condemnation. He offered forgiveness and a call to change. In addiction, we often stand in self-condemnation. Imagine the Savior standing by you, dispersing the inner critics, then gently saying, "I don't condemn you; let's move forward together." That's the heart of the gospel—hope for transformation rather than a verdict of permanent failure.

It's also helpful to remember that there's a difference between temptation and sin. Being tempted is not a sin. Even Jesus was tempted (Matthew 4:1, KJV). Many people with addictions are bombarded by temptation daily, and they might mistakenly believe they're sinning just by feeling that pull. But sin enters when we yield to temptation. Learning to differentiate between the two can free us from unnecessary guilt. We can say, "Lord, I'm feeling tempted, and I hate this feeling, but I'm coming to You for strength to resist." That's a faithful response, and it's entirely different from giving in.

Don't discount small victories. Maybe you went one more day clean than last time, or you prayed immediately when the craving hit, or you reached out to a friend instead of isolating. Each of those victories, no matter how small, matters to the Lord. He sees your effort. He rejoices in each step you take toward Him. Sometimes we think spirituality is all or nothing, but the gospel is about progression. Elder Dale G. Renlund compared the Savior to a loving physician who will give us the perfect prescription for our condition (Renlund, 2015, p. 100). That prescription might include consistent prayer, reading the scriptures, support groups, and heartfelt repentance. He personalizes the treatment plan for each of us, and He celebrates every step we take on the path to recovery.

When the darkness of addiction feels overwhelming, remember that Jesus is often found in dark places. He was born in a humble stable, prayed alone in Gethsemane at night, and was laid in a sealed tomb before rising in glorious resurrection. He knows darkness intimately—yet He is the Light of the World (John 8:12, KJV). Invite that Light into your personal darkness, even if it's just a flicker at first. Over time, as you continue inviting

Him in, that light will grow stronger. It might reveal messy corners of your life that need cleaning, but it will also reveal your divine potential and God's unwavering belief in you.

It helps to keep an eternal perspective. This life, while crucial, is not the whole story. God's commitment to our growth spans beyond mortality. If you keep striving, keep repenting, and keep trusting in His grace, you'll find that addiction doesn't get the final word. The final word belongs to the Savior who overcame all things. In the Book of Revelation, we find the promise that God will wipe away all tears and make all things new (Revelation 21:4–5, KJV). That includes renewing our bodies, minds, and spirits in ways we can't fully comprehend right now. No matter how entrenched you feel in your addiction, no matter how many times you've stumbled, that divine renewal is available to you.

I realize talk is cheap when you're in the thick of addiction. But I also know that living prophets, apostles, and many modern Christian leaders speak consistently about hope in Christ because they've seen real miracles—miracles of changed hearts, restored relationships, and lasting freedom. Those aren't just sentimental stories; they're evidence of a living Savior who is still very much in the business of saving souls. Elder Dieter F. Uchtdorf once said, "We can't go back in time and change the past, but we can repent. The Savior can wipe away our tears of regret" (Uchtdorf, 2007, p. 99). Imagine that—having your tears of regret replaced with tears of gratitude. That's the journey we embark on when we let the Savior into our addiction story.

If there's one thought I want to leave with you, it's this: do not give up on yourself, because God certainly hasn't. He is bigger than your addiction, stronger than your cravings, and infinitely more patient than your harshest self-critic. You might feel stuck in a cycle today, but that cycle can be broken. Keep turning to the scriptures. Keep turning to prayer. Keep seeking professional help if needed. Keep surrounding yourself with people who lift you rather than pull you down. Keep knocking on heaven's door. Eventually, that door swings wide, revealing that God has been on the other side all along, eagerly waiting to embrace you in love and show you the path to freedom.

At some point, you'll look back and see how far you've come. Yes, there might be scars—physical, emotional, spiritual. But those scars can become symbols of triumph, reminding you of the time God's grace worked a mighty change in your life. In that sense, your addiction story can become a story of redemption, inspiring others who feel hopeless. You'll be able to testify firsthand that Jesus Christ isn't just a figure in ancient scripture—He is a living Savior who rescues real people in modern times, one struggling heart at a time.

So hold on. Keep faith. And remember: you are a beloved child of Heavenly Father. Nothing can separate you from the love of God which is in Christ Jesus (Romans 8:38–39, KJV). Not addiction, not shame, not relapses, not the voices that say you'll never change. His love is unwavering, and it's your lifeline. Let that lifeline tug you upward, one day at a time, until you stand on solid ground once more. He believes in you. And so do I
.

Chapter 4: When Loneliness Feels Overwhelming

Loneliness can feel like a giant echo chamber where it seems our thoughts bounce around, growing louder with each pass. It's that ache in our chest when we wake up and realize we aren't excited to face the day, or when we come home to an empty house and no one asks how our day went. It's also possible to feel lonely even when we're surrounded by people—because loneliness isn't always about the absence of company; it's about the absence of connection. If that's where you find yourself—feeling isolated, misunderstood, or just plain invisible—please know you are not alone in the eyes of Heavenly Father. His love is real, and His awareness of you is deeply personal. My hope is that by the time you finish this chapter, you'll sense even a flicker of light in that darkness, remembering that Jesus Christ is not a distant figure in a painting, but a living Savior who longs to ease your burdens and fill your heart with belonging.

Maybe you've wondered why God allows us to feel lonely at all. Wouldn't life be easier if we were always surrounded by supportive friends and family, never lacking for companionship? Perhaps. But there's something about feeling lonely that can also drive us into a deeper relationship with our Heavenly Father if we let it. Instead of turning inward and replaying how isolated we feel, we can try turning upward, acknowledging the emptiness and asking God to fill it. One of my favorite reminders is in Psalm 34:18, which says, "The Lord is nigh unto them that are of a broken heart; and saveth such as be of a contrite spirit" (KJV). If loneliness has broken your heart, you fit that description perfectly. The Lord is near you. He doesn't roll His eyes at your sadness or tell you to "just get over it." He draws close, ready to comfort and uplift.

It might be hard to sense that closeness when you feel alone. But think of it like radio waves—they're constantly around us, but we need a receiver tuned in to pick them up. Sometimes, the receiver of our heart needs quiet moments of prayer, scripture study, or just honest conversation with God. Talk to Him like you would a best friend: "Heavenly Father, I'm lonely. I feel like nobody understands me. I need Your help to see that I'm not by myself." This kind of candid prayer can crack open a window of hope. Sure, it might not instantly solve every social woe or heal every rift, but it's the start of inviting the most powerful and loving Being in the universe to walk with you.

Jesus Himself experienced loneliness in a profound way. The scriptures tell us that in the Garden of Gethsemane, even His closest disciples fell asleep while He suffered (Matthew 26:38–40, KJV). And on the cross, He cried out, "My God, my God, why hast thou forsaken me?" (Matthew 27:46, KJV). Whether we interpret that literally or as an expression of unimaginable agony, the point is that the Savior knows the sting of feeling alone. He isn't remote from our experience—He's lived it. Because He knows that pain firsthand, He also knows how to comfort us in it (Alma

7:11–12, Book of Mormon). That's not just a Sunday School platitude. It's a promise from a Savior who walked a path of suffering to ensure we'd never be truly abandoned.

Now, if loneliness is your constant companion, you might wonder if you're somehow defective. Let me assure you: being lonely doesn't mean you're broken; it means you're human. We are social creatures by divine design—Heavenly Father declared that it's "not good" for us to be alone (Genesis 2:18, KJV). So it's normal to crave companionship. The real question is, how do we handle this season of loneliness in a healthy, Christ-centered way? Sometimes we try to numb it with distractions—endless scrolling on social media or binge-watching TV shows. While those might offer temporary relief, they seldom address the deeper longing for real, meaningful connection.

Connection can be cultivated in many ways. Prayer is one. Scripture study is another. But there's also something to be said for seeking out human relationships, even if it feels scary. The adversary loves to convince us that nobody wants us around, or that we're too awkward or too flawed to be loved. Those are lies. God created you with unique gifts and a capacity to bless others, and there are people out there who need what only you can offer—your perspective, your kindness, your sense of humor, your empathy. So, if loneliness has led you to isolate yourself further, consider taking a small step outward. Volunteer somewhere. Show up to a community class or activity that aligns with your interests. Join a local church group if you're comfortable, or a support group for people wrestling with similar feelings. You might be surprised to find others longing for connection just as much as you are.

That said, some of us carry a deeper kind of loneliness that stems from past hurts—maybe a betrayal, a strained family relationship, or repeated rejections. We might feel safer keeping everyone at arm's length because letting people in risks getting hurt again. But here's a gentle reminder: closing our hearts for protection can also lock out the possibility of real friendship and love. Yes, it's risky to open up, but it's also an act of faith. Elder Jeffrey R. Holland once said, "Hope on. Journey on" (Holland, 2013, p. 42). Part of hoping and journeying is believing that despite past disappointments, there can still be genuine connections in our future.

One of the greatest examples of overcoming loneliness with divine help is the prophet Joseph Smith. He was a young boy searching for truth, and he felt alone in his quest (Joseph Smith—History 1:8, The Church of Jesus Christ of Latter-day Saints). Yet he turned to prayer, believing that God could answer him personally. When Heavenly Father and Jesus Christ appeared to him in what we call the First Vision, Joseph's life changed. He wasn't alone in his questions anymore. Likewise, we can take our deepest questions and longings to the Lord in prayer, trusting He will guide us in ways that may not be as dramatic as the First Vision, but can be just as personally meaningful.

In moments when the loneliness becomes overwhelming, another powerful tool is gratitude. I know, that might sound cliché—"Just count your blessings!"—but hear me out. When we make a conscious effort to notice what's going right (even if it's something small like a warm bed or a ray of sunshine), we can shift our focus from what's missing to what's present. President Russell M. Nelson taught that heartfelt gratitude can help us see God's hand in our lives more clearly (Nelson, 2020, p. 28). Gradually, that awareness can remind us we're never as alone as our emotions might suggest.

It's also worth mentioning that loneliness can sometimes be a clue from our spirit that we need to deepen our relationship with God. Elder Dieter

F. Uchtdorf said that we are "spiritual beings having a mortal experience" (Uchtdorf, 2010, p. 86). If our spiritual needs aren't being met—if we're neglecting prayer, scripture study, or service—we might feel a spiritual emptiness that we mislabel as loneliness. By reconnecting with Heavenly Father, we often find that some of that ache lifts. It doesn't necessarily remove our desire for human companionship, but it provides a foundation of divine comfort that can help us endure seasons of solitude with a little more grace.

Now, I don't want to gloss over the fact that sometimes loneliness is wrapped up in mental health struggles like depression or anxiety. If you suspect that may be the case, please don't hesitate to seek professional help. Just as we'd see a doctor for a persistent fever, it's wise to talk to a therapist or counselor when persistent loneliness or sadness starts affecting our daily life. Heavenly Father often answers our prayers by guiding us to professionals who have the knowledge to help us navigate these complex emotional landscapes. You don't have to do this alone. Seeking help is a sign of strength, not weakness.

We also can't ignore the reality that in today's digital age, a lot of our "connections" happen online. While social media can be a blessing, it can also create comparison traps that deepen our loneliness. We scroll through highlight reels of other people's lives and think, "Why is everyone else so happy and surrounded by friends?" But remember, social media rarely shows the full picture. You might be comparing your behind-the-scenes struggles with someone else's heavily edited snapshots. Instead of dwelling on what others appear to have, consider investing time in real-life connections—calling a friend, writing a letter, or volunteering in person.

If you find yourself discouraged because the loneliness hasn't lifted yet, take courage in knowing that every chapter of life is temporary. Elder Neal A. Maxwell once said, "Faith in God includes faith in His timing" (Maxwell, 1991, p. 76). We don't know exactly when our season of loneliness will end or how it will shift, but we can trust that God's plan for us is loving. Sometimes He allows us to walk through solitary valleys because there's growth and compassion to be gained there—compassion we can later offer someone else who feels alone. Other times, He blesses us with an unexpected friendship or an opportunity to serve that changes everything. The key is to keep our eyes open for those blessings.

One practical idea is to look for ways to serve others, even in small acts. It might seem counterintuitive when we're feeling lonely to focus on someone else's needs, but service often helps break the cycle of self-focus that loneliness perpetuates. Mosiah 2:17 (Book of Mormon) teaches that "when ye are in the service of your fellow beings ye are only in the service of your God." As we lift others, the Spirit of the Lord can lift us in return. It's not a magic trick that instantly cures loneliness, but it does remind us we have something to offer the world—and that realization can plant seeds of belonging in our hearts.

Another thing to consider is that loneliness can sometimes be a wake-up call to reconcile important relationships. Perhaps there's been a falling-out with a family member or friend. If so, take that to the Lord in prayer. Ask if there's a step you can take to mend that bridge. Not all broken relationships can or should be repaired—sometimes boundaries are essential for our well-being. But if there's a misunderstanding or pride that's kept you apart from someone you care about, loneliness might be the nudge to say, "Let's fix this if we can." Even if the other person doesn't respond, you can at least find peace knowing you tried.

Sometimes, we look at loneliness as a punishment, but what if we saw it as an invitation? An invitation from the Lord to get to know Him better, to discover who we really are, and to clarify what we want from life. There's a difference between being alone and being lonely. Being alone can be a fruitful time if we use it to grow closer to God and to reflect on our purposes and goals. Elder Henry B. Eyring once said, "If you are on the right path, it will always be uphill" (Eyring, 2002, p. 109). Sometimes the climb is solitary, but it doesn't mean we're off track. It might mean Heavenly Father is preparing us for something that requires a season of quiet growth.

If you're feeling like the walls are closing in, remember that the Savior is often found in lonely places. After all, He was born in a humble stable, prayed alone in Gethsemane, and spent forty days in the wilderness. Time and again, He showed us that holy moments can occur in isolation. When we invite Him into our loneliness, that space can become hallowed ground. Instead of a prison cell, our solitude can become a sanctuary where we commune deeply with our Maker, receiving comfort and direction that we might miss in the hustle and bustle of busier times.

And if you ever doubt whether you truly matter, recall the parable of the lost sheep (Luke 15:4–7, KJV). The Shepherd left the ninety-nine to find the one. That's how singularly important you are to Him. You are the one He seeks when you wander, the one He calls by name, the one He carries home on His shoulders. If you feel lost in loneliness, He is on His way to you—maybe in subtle ways, maybe through a friend's text or a scripture that suddenly speaks to your heart. Keep your eyes open for those tender mercies. They're like little breadcrumbs leading you back to the realization that you are not forgotten and never could be, not by the One who created your very soul.

My hope is that as you continue reading and praying, some of that loneliness will begin to lift, or at least feel more bearable. Don't give up if it lingers. Remember, you're in a conversation with the God of the universe, and He has a perfect track record of turning mourning into dancing (Psalm 30:11, KJV). It might not happen overnight, but hold on to hope. Allow yourself moments of rest in His presence, whether that's through heartfelt prayer, meditating on His words, or letting a favorite hymn wash over you. Those spiritual practices aren't quick fixes, but they're lifelines to a Heavenly Father who deeply desires to pour out His love upon you.

If you can, reach out to someone today. Send a text, make a call, offer a kind word. Even if you're the one feeling lonely, you might be surprised how reaching out to someone else can ease your own ache. And if you don't receive the response you hoped for, don't let that discourage you. Keep trying, keep praying for guidance, and trust that God sees your efforts. In His eyes, no act of compassion goes unnoticed or unrewarded.

Your loneliness doesn't define you; it's a season, a feeling, not your identity. You are a child of God, cherished by Jesus Christ, and enveloped in a grand plan that includes joy, relationships, and meaningful connections. As you walk through this chapter of loneliness, let the Savior walk beside you. Talk to Him as you would a friend, and let His presence remind you that you are never, ever truly alone. That's not just wishful thinking—it's the gospel truth, sealed by the blood and tears of a Savior who has promised He will never leave us comfortless (John 14:18, KJV).

I testify that Jesus Christ cares about your loneliness. He cares about every tear you shed in secret. And I promise that as you turn to Him, you'll find subtle and sometimes surprising ways in which He soothes your heart. Hang on. Keep believing. Better days are coming, and even while you wait, you can discover moments of divine peace. Let Him hold you in that peace, and remember that you are His cherished child, no matter how alone you feel in the world. He is near, He is real, and He will never forsake you.

Chapter 5: Understanding God's Plan for You

If you've ever felt lost or aimless in life, you're certainly not alone. Many of us wonder: "Why am I here? Does Heavenly Father really have a plan for someone like me? And if He does, how do I fit into it?" These questions can weigh heavy on our minds, especially when we're struggling. But the incredible news is that yes—there is a plan, and you have a vital role to play within it. In fact, you're so important to God that He formed a blueprint for your spiritual growth and happiness long before you took your first breath on this earth. That's not just a cozy idea; it's a life-altering truth that can anchor us when storms hit.

Sometimes we hear phrases like "God's Plan of Happiness" or "Plan of Salvation," and they sound huge and abstract. But in essence, the plan is about family, love, growth, and returning to live with Heavenly Father. Part of that plan involved our coming to earth, receiving a physical body, and being tested in a world where we have the agency to choose right from wrong. It's also about having a Savior—Jesus Christ—who makes it possible for us to overcome sin and even death, through His Atonement and Resurrection. When you really think about it, that's not just cosmic theology; it's the ultimate rescue mission. Jesus volunteered to be our Advocate, bridging the gap between our weaknesses and God's holiness (2 Nephi 2:6–8, Book of Mormon). That's how precious you are in His sight.

But what about the nitty-gritty details of our individual paths? What about the specific struggles, disappointments, and detours we face? That's where trusting God's timing and methods becomes essential. Jeremiah 29:11 (KJV) reassures us that God knows the plans He has for us—plans to give us hope and a future. Sometimes, though, our personal journey feels so chaotic that we wonder if there was ever a plan at all. Perhaps we've made poor choices, or maybe life has simply dished out more trials than we think we can handle. Let me remind you that none of your trials take God by surprise. He's never thrown off balance by your setbacks. He can weave even your biggest mistakes into a tapestry of growth, if you'll let Him.

That doesn't mean He orchestrates every hardship in our lives. People have agency, and sometimes that means they make choices that hurt us. Other times, mortality itself hands us challenges like illness, accidents, or natural disasters. But the promise of the gospel is that no experience is wasted if we bring it to Jesus Christ. He can transform our pain into empathy, our mistakes into wisdom, and our heartbreak into humility. Elder Dieter F. Uchtdorf said, "God is fully aware that you and I are not perfect. Let me add: God is also fully aware that the people you think are perfect are not" (Uchtdorf, 2012, p. 22). That quote makes me smile because it's so true—God's plan doesn't hinge on our perfection; it hinges on our willingness to keep trying, repenting, and learning.

One stumbling block can be our own limited perspective. We might think, "I'm not serving a mission, or I'm not married, or I don't have a successful career. I must be off track." But that's not always how God sees it. The plan is broad enough to accommodate endless variations of righteous paths. If you're earnestly doing your best—trying to follow Christ, repenting when you fall, loving others, and seeking to serve—then you're very much on His path for you. Elder Neal A. Maxwell once said that God doesn't just want us to "go through" trials; He wants us to "grow through" them (Maxwell, 1990, p. 12). Every piece of your life's puzzle can help you become more like your Heavenly Father if you choose to let it.

It can help to look at scriptural examples of God working with imperfect, struggling people to accomplish His grand designs. Moses doubted his ability to lead. Peter denied knowing the Savior three times. Alma the Younger was essentially an enemy to the Church before his dramatic conversion (Mosiah 27:8–24, Book of Mormon). And yet, these flawed individuals became remarkable instruments in God's hands. Their stories testify that divine potential is not reserved for the superhuman—it's available to each of us. The same God who guided them guides you. And Jesus Christ, who forgave them, will forgive you—no matter how many times you've stumbled.

But how do we discern our place in this plan on a day-to-day level? Sometimes we want a detailed map with every turn labeled, but God often provides just enough light for the next step (Psalm 119:105, KJV). That's where prayer, scripture study, and personal revelation come in. As we consistently seek the Lord's will, we become more attuned to the gentle nudges of the Holy Spirit. Those nudges might come as thoughts, feelings, or promptings we can't quite explain logically, but they press upon our hearts in a way that feels holy. When you sense one of those promptings—maybe to reach out to a friend, pursue a new job, or simply be more patient—try acting on it. Over time, you'll see how those small acts of obedience gradually unveil the path God has prepared for you.

Sometimes, we fear we'll mess up God's plan if we make a wrong turn. That's a heavy burden to carry, and it's also not accurate. Of course, our choices matter, and some decisions can lead us away from blessings we might have received sooner. But remember, God is the Master Planner. He knows every contingency. He can open new doors when others close. He can line up resources, people, and experiences that bring us back to His path, even if we've meandered for years. Think of Jonah, who literally ran the opposite direction of what God asked him to do, ended up in the belly of a fish, and still accomplished the mission God had for him (Jonah 1–3, KJV). If God can work with Jonah, He can certainly work with us.

Of course, that doesn't mean we should slack off or live recklessly. The plan isn't an excuse to be idle; it's a motivator to keep learning and growing. President Russell M. Nelson taught that we have "divine potential" and that our Heavenly Father "wants us to grow and achieve our potential" (Nelson, 2017, p. 35). That growth often comes through challenges. Have you ever noticed how a plant has to push through the soil to reach the sunlight? Likewise, we often have to push through adversity to discover just how strong, faithful, and resilient we can be. Sometimes that feels unfair—especially when we're already struggling. But adversity can also be a catalyst for breakthroughs. It's in those moments of stretching that we learn to rely on Christ in ways that transform us.

One aspect of God's plan that can be hard to grasp is timing. We might watch friends or family members achieve their goals while we wait and wonder, "When is it my turn?" This can breed impatience, envy, or discouragement. But each person's story unfolds differently. Elder Holland once said, "Some blessings come soon, some come late, and some don't come until heaven" (Holland, 1999, p. 38). That's a tough pill to swallow when our hearts are aching for an answer right now. But if we trust that God loves us perfectly, we can also trust that He knows the best timing to grant blessings—or to withhold them for a season so we can learn and become more than we are.

Another comforting truth is that our Savior is deeply invested in our individual journey. He's not just interested in big, dramatic changes—He's interested in every baby step we take toward righteousness. That's because the plan isn't about simply checking off boxes; it's about the gradual shaping of our hearts. If you've ever molded clay, you know the process takes patience. The Potter gently shapes, re-shapes, adds water when needed, and smooths rough edges. Isaiah 64:8 says, "We are the clay, and thou our potter" (KJV). We can trust the Master Potter to shape us into something beautiful—even if at times we feel squished and molded in uncomfortable ways.

What if you're in a season where you just can't see God's plan at all? Maybe your life is full of conflict, loss, or seemingly endless closed doors. In those moments, it's okay to have questions. It's okay to cry out, "God, why is this happening?" The scriptures are filled with people who brought their frustrations to the Lord. Take the prophet Habakkuk, for example—his entire book starts with a lament about the injustices around him (Habakkuk 1:2–4, KJV). Yet God eventually revealed His purposes, and Habakkuk concluded with a powerful declaration of trust (Habakkuk 3:17–19, KJV). That's often how it goes: we wrestle, we wonder, and then, in God's timing, clarity comes. Sometimes that clarity is immediate, and sometimes it's delayed, but whenever it arrives, it brings peace that surpasses mere logic.

A crucial part of discovering God's plan is remembering that He respects our agency. He might prompt us, guide us, and even warn us, but He won't force us to follow. Our willingness to choose Him, to choose righteousness, is central to the entire plan. That's why the Book of Mormon repeatedly emphasizes that "ye are free; ye are permitted to act for yourselves" (Helaman 14:30). Agency is a gift, but it comes with responsibility. God loves us enough to let us learn from our choices, both good and bad. Even when we choose poorly, He doesn't abandon us—He patiently waits for us to realize our mistake and come back.

It's also important to realize that God's plan is not just about us as individuals—it's about our relationships. Families, friendships, and church communities are part of the plan. We grow together, we learn to forgive, we learn to serve. That's why cultivating healthy relationships matters. If you've been hurt or isolated, it might feel risky to engage in fellowship again, but the journey of discipleship isn't meant to be traveled alone. We can look to Jesus, who surrounded Himself with disciples and friends, sharing meals, praying with them, and teaching them. Even in His darkest hours, He invited a select few to watch with Him (Matthew 26:36–38, KJV). That relational aspect is woven into the plan—it teaches us empathy, patience, and love.

Now, if you're reading this and feeling like you've strayed too far from God's plan, I want to remind you that the plan includes the Atonement for a reason. There is no point of no return with Jesus Christ. Alma the Younger was described as "the very vilest of sinners" (Mosiah 28:4, Book of Mormon), yet through repentance and God's mercy, he became one of the greatest missionaries in scripture. That's not just a neat storyline—it's a demonstration of how powerful grace can be. Whatever your past, you can step back onto the covenant path. And every step you take forward is celebrated by angels (Luke 15:10, KJV).

It might help to pray specifically for eyes to see the plan. Say something like, "Heavenly Father, please help me understand how my life fits into Your eternal purposes. Open my heart to the lessons I'm supposed to learn right now." That prayer shows a willingness to be taught. Sometimes the answers come in a Sunday sermon, a conversation with a friend, or even a quiet moment where your thoughts suddenly feel crystal clear. President Boyd K. Packer once said, "The Spirit does not get our attention by shouting or shaking us with a heavy hand. Rather, it whispers" (Packer, 1983, p. 66). Be prepared for subtlety. God often speaks in still, small voices rather than thunderclaps.

Another angle to consider is that discovering God's plan doesn't guarantee an easy life. Jesus Himself said, "In the world ye shall have tribulation" (John 16:33, KJV). The difference is that when we walk in God's plan, our trials become stepping-stones instead of stumbling blocks. They refine us into Christlike individuals. We learn patience when we face delays, empathy when we endure hardships, and faith when we're forced to rely on God. Over time, we come to see that a life aligned with His will—though not free of pain—brings a deep sense of purpose that outweighs the momentary afflictions.

In practical terms, living God's plan might look like daily prayer, consistent scripture study, serving in your local congregation, or quietly performing acts of kindness. It might mean letting go of habits that keep you from the Spirit—whether that's cynicism, procrastination, or unhealthy behaviors. It may involve big, life-changing decisions like going to college, changing jobs, or moving to a new area. In all these things, the invitation is to involve the Lord. Ask for guidance. Consult the scriptures.

Counsel with trusted mentors. Then make the best decision you can and move forward, trusting that if you need to pivot, God will make it clear.

Ultimately, understanding God's plan is about understanding our identity. We're not random accidents; we're beloved spirit children of a Heavenly Father who wants us back home, changed and sanctified by our earthly journey. And we have a Savior who voluntarily paved the way for that return through His infinite sacrifice. Everything—every sorrow, every joy, every disappointment—can be consecrated for our good (Romans 8:28, KJV). Knowing that can transform how we see our challenges. We realize life isn't just happening to us; it's happening for us, in the sense that each experience can shape us into who God knows we can become.

If you're in a dark place, unsure if any of this applies to you, hold on to the fact that God's plan is real even when we can't see it. Just because clouds cover the sun doesn't mean the sun has ceased to exist. Sometimes, we're in a cloudy season, but the Son—Jesus Christ—is still there, shining His light of truth and love on us. We just need to keep walking forward, trusting that the clouds will part, and we'll see more clearly when the time is right.

I testify that you have a divine purpose. Heavenly Father didn't send you here just to wander aimlessly. Your life matters, your struggles matter, and your victories matter. And no matter how twisted or unexpected your path has been, you're still in the story, and God is still writing. The plan is bigger than our limited view. Let that truth settle into your heart and give you hope. Let it remind you that you are cherished beyond measure, and that in the grand unfolding of God's work, you have a crucial role that only you can fill. It might not be glamorous; it might not be noticed by the world. But it is precious in His sight. Keep learning, keep trusting, keep moving forward with faith in Jesus Christ. One day, you'll look back and realize that every twist and turn was leading you closer to the glorious destiny God envisioned for you all along.

Chapter 6: Finding Strength With Others

Picture yourself standing on a hilltop. You're tired, bruised, and maybe a little discouraged—life has been throwing curveballs left and right. Suddenly, you look around and notice you're not alone. Others are standing with you, extending a hand or offering a shoulder to lean on. Their eyes say, "We're in this together." That's the vision I want us to explore: finding real strength in a community of caring, Christ-centered people who remind us that we don't have to go through life's struggles by ourselves. Heavenly Father never intended for us to live in complete isolation. While solitary prayer and personal reflection have their place, there is an undeniable power that comes from gathering with fellow believers and friends, lifting one another's burdens, and rejoicing in one another's triumphs.

It might help to remember that Jesus set this example Himself. He didn't just preach to crowds; He formed relationships. He called disciples, broke bread with them, and shared in their joys and sorrows. Think about how many miracles He performed while surrounded by friends or curious onlookers. Even in His darkest hours, like in Gethsemane, He invited Peter, James, and John to be near Him (Matthew 26:36–38, King James Version). Though they fell asleep, His request still shows us something important: the Son of God, who could command angels if He wished, valued the presence of fellow humans in His hardest moments. If Jesus valued community, maybe we can see it as more than just a "nice option" but as an essential part of a healthy spiritual life.

Sometimes, we shy away from community because people can be messy. Churches and friend groups aren't made up of perfect individuals; they're made up of real people with quirks, weaknesses, and yes, sometimes they can let us down. But the Lord never asked us to form perfect communities—He asked us to form loving ones. He said, "By this shall all men know that ye are my disciples, if ye have love one to another" (John 13:35, KJV). That love is the glue that holds communities together when misunderstandings or offenses threaten to tear them apart. If you've been hurt by someone in a church or group setting, please know that the Savior sees your pain and wants you to heal. Don't let one painful experience make you swear off the gift of fellowship altogether. The adversary would love for us to isolate ourselves based on a single negative interaction. But God invites us to keep reaching out, keep forgiving, and keep searching for the good.

One of the great benefits of a supportive community is accountability. When we're struggling, whether it's with a personal weakness or a heavy trial, having friends who check in can make all the difference. If you've ever tried to reach a goal—like overcoming an addiction, improving your prayer life, or even losing weight—you know that doing it alone can feel impossible. But when someone walks alongside you, cheering you on, everything shifts. Instead of an uphill climb by yourself, it becomes a shared journey. Galatians 6:2 tells us to "bear ye one another's burdens" (KJV). That's not just a polite suggestion; it's a powerful principle that can bring relief to weary hearts. When we carry each other's loads, no single person collapses under the weight.

If you're reading this and thinking, "But my church experience has been anything but uplifting," I get that. Churches are run by imperfect humans, and it's possible you encountered judgment, gossip, or indifference. Let me suggest a different perspective. Could it be that Heavenly Father might lead you to a congregation where your presence, with all your experiences and compassion, is exactly what someone else needs? You might become the person who greets newcomers warmly, or who extends a listening ear to someone going through a crisis. What if your past hurts can be transformed into a testimony of empathy that blesses others? Elder Dieter F. Uchtdorf once taught that "the Church is not an automobile showroom—a place to put ourselves on display so others can admire our spirituality… It is more like a service center, where… we work together to help each other" (Uchtdorf, 2014, p. 56). That means your church family can be a workshop of healing and growth. Yes, mistakes will happen, but grace can abound all the more.

Community doesn't only happen within the walls of a church building. It can also flourish in small groups, circles of friends, online forums, or service projects. The key ingredient is genuine connection centered on uplifting one another in faith and love. If you're blessed with a circle of believing friends, cherish that gift. Pray for each other, study scriptures together, and be real about your struggles. Vulnerability can be scary—we might worry about judgment—but authentic sharing often opens the door to deeper support. James 5:16 reminds us, "Confess your faults one to another, and pray one for another, that ye may be healed" (KJV). Being honest about our shortcomings can actually strengthen the bonds of fellowship, because everyone realizes they're not alone in their imperfections.

Of course, building community requires more than just showing up on a Sunday or occasionally texting a friend. It takes intentional effort. For some of us, that might mean stepping out of our comfort zones. Think about the Good Samaritan (Luke 10:25–37, KJV). He could have easily passed by the wounded man, just like the priest and Levite did. But he chose to stop, bind the man's wounds, and invest real time and resources into helping him. That's a glimpse of true community—seeing a need, responding to it, and in the process discovering that caring for someone else also enriches our own soul. When we reach out consistently, we plant seeds of trust and friendship that grow into a strong network of support.

You might wonder, "What if I'm too broken or too socially awkward to be part of a community?" But here's the beautiful paradox: community is often the best remedy for our perceived weaknesses. Elder Jeffrey R. Holland once reminded us that "imperfect people are all God has ever had to work with. That must be terribly frustrating to Him, but He deals with it. So should we" (Holland, 2013, p. 43). You don't need to be perfect to belong. In fact, admitting our flaws and struggles can be the very thing that helps us find authentic belonging, because others who've been holding their own struggles silently suddenly realize it's safe to open up. When we show up with our vulnerabilities, we often invite others to do the same.

Another advantage of community is the collective wisdom it offers. When you face a dilemma—spiritual, financial, emotional, or otherwise—you can glean insights from those who've walked a similar path. Maybe someone in your congregation overcame a similar trial and can share how God carried them through. Maybe an older mentor has a calm perspective that you haven't considered. Proverbs 11:14 teaches that "in the multitude of counsellors there is safety" (KJV). That doesn't mean we blindly follow everyone's advice, but it does mean we can prayerfully consider the experiences and counsel of those around us, trusting that God might use them as instruments in our healing and guidance.

For those who feel hesitant because they've been let down by communities in the past, consider starting fresh with prayer. Ask Heavenly Father to guide you to a place—or a group of people—where you can serve, grow, and find mutual support. Then act on any promptings you receive. It might be intimidating, but remember, progress often happens on the other side of our comfort zone. If the first (or second, or third) community setting doesn't feel right, don't lose hope. Keep seeking. Keep praying. The Lord honors persistent faith. He knows how crucial fellowship is for our well-being.

Sometimes, people say, "But I have God—that's all I need." And while it's true that a relationship with Jesus Christ is the ultimate anchor, He often blesses us through other people. Paul wrote extensively about the metaphor of the Church being like a body (1 Corinthians 12:12–27, KJV). Each part has its unique function, but they need each other to form a healthy, living whole. Imagine if the hand said, "I don't need the rest of the body," or the foot declared, "I can walk this journey alone." That wouldn't just be foolish; it would be detrimental. There's a reason the Lord established a community of believers. We refine each other, learn from each other, and become more like Christ as we practice real-life discipleship side by side.

If you're looking for ways to strengthen the community you already have, start small. Offer a genuine compliment. Ask someone how they're really doing, and then listen without interruption. Volunteer your time or talents—even if it's something as simple as greeting people at the door. Offer to pray with someone who's struggling. These might seem like small gestures, but they create an atmosphere of belonging that can transform a group of acquaintances into a family of faith. President Russell M. Nelson explained that "the highest and noblest work in this life is that of a ministering angel. We can bless others in so many ways as we reach out in love and kindness" (Nelson, 1996, p. 14). As we do, we'll find our own burdens feeling lighter because we're no longer consumed by our own troubles alone.

Community also thrives when we learn to celebrate each other's victories. In a world that sometimes fosters competition and envy, let's be the type of people who genuinely rejoice when a friend gets a promotion, recovers from illness, or has a family milestone. Romans 12:15 instructs us to "rejoice with them that do rejoice, and weep with them that weep" (KJV). Both are forms of empathy, and both create deeper connections. When we celebrate together, we multiply the joy. When we mourn together, we divide the sorrow. That's the beauty of a spiritually alive community.

Of course, not everyone's personality leans naturally toward socializing. Some of us are introverts, and large gatherings drain our energy. That's okay. Community doesn't have to be big to be meaningful. Even a tight-knit circle of two or three trusted friends can form a powerful support system. The scriptures promise that "where two or three are gathered together in my name, there am I in the midst of them" (Matthew 18:20, KJV). So if big groups intimidate you, focus on cultivating a few close relationships. The point is not to force yourself into a mold but to recognize that God works wonders through relationships, and each one of us needs that lifeline of fellowship in one form or another.

Let's also address the potential for disappointment within communities. Because people are human, conflicts can arise. We might feel sidelined or misunderstood at times. In those instances, it's vital to remember that our relationship with Christ should anchor us above all else. We belong to communities not because they're flawless, but because they help us grow and serve. When friction happens, we have a chance to practice forgiveness, patience, and humility—traits Jesus modeled so perfectly. Elder David A. Bednar taught that "the capacity to love, serve, and forgive others is an ongoing daily challenge and [an] opportunity" (Bednar, 2016, p. 55). Communities can be a spiritual laboratory where we test and refine these virtues.

Another aspect of community is accountability to spiritual leaders or mentors. For instance, talking to a pastor, bishop, or relief society president (if you're in an LDS context) about your struggles can open doors to resources or counseling that you never knew existed. Don't let pride or fear keep you from seeking that support. Leaders are called to serve, and while they aren't perfect, many have a deep desire to lift and guide. They can also connect you with programs for mental health, addiction recovery, or financial assistance if you're in crisis. God's work is often done through the hands of those who've been called to minister.

At the end of the day, community is about recognizing that we are the body of Christ—united by our love for Him, shaped by our hope in His gospel, and led by His Spirit. None of us have all the answers, but together we can puzzle out solutions, offer comfort, and remind each other of eternal truths when life gets overwhelming. If you've been in a spiritual slump, or if your faith feels fragile, a community of faithful friends might be the scaffolding you need while you rebuild. If you're feeling strong, then your community needs you to help shore up someone else's weakness. It's a beautiful, reciprocal cycle that knits hearts together in love.

Let me share a personal note: some of my sweetest spiritual experiences have come not from solitary study but from group discussions and heartfelt testimonies shared with friends. There's something about hearing another person's struggle and seeing how the Lord carried them that builds my faith. It's like a puzzle piece clicking into place, reminding me that if God was there for them, He'll be there for me too. We read in Doctrine and Covenants 6:32, "Where two or three are gathered together in my name… behold, there will I be" (The Church of Jesus Christ of Latter-day Saints, 2013). That presence can be tangible—the comforting reassurance of the Holy Spirit, binding us together and testifying that Jesus Christ is real, and that we matter to Him.

So how do we take all these ideas and turn them into action? Start by praying specifically for opportunities to build or join a Christ-centered community. Ask the Lord to guide you, then be ready to act on promptings. If you feel nudged to invite someone to a Bible study or to sit with you at church, do it. If you sense you should call an old friend who's been on your mind, pick up the phone. If your community has a service project, jump in with both feet. These small yeses to the Lord often lead to bigger blessings than we ever anticipated. Over time, you may find that your circle of believers grows richer, and your own testimony grows deeper, all because you chose to link arms with fellow travelers on this earthly journey.

Community can't fix every problem, but it can lighten almost any load. It might not remove your trials, but it can help you face them with courage. And in those moments when you feel your strength is at an end, a loving friend or fellow church member might remind you to look up, to trust

God, and to take one more step. That's the gospel in action—Christ's love reflected in ordinary people who care enough to walk alongside each other.

I promise that as you seek and nurture Christ-centered community, you'll witness small miracles—someone will say exactly what you need to hear, or you'll find yourself comforting someone else with words you didn't realize you had. You'll see hearts soften, relationships mend, and burdens shared. Most importantly, you'll catch glimpses of the Savior's own loving heart, because whenever we unite in His name, He draws near. In a world that can feel increasingly divided and disconnected, a true, loving community is a treasure. May you discover or help create one that reminds you daily that you are known, valued, and never alone.

Chapter 7: Healing the Broken Heart

Let's talk about heartbreak and grief—the sort of pain that makes it hard to breathe when you first wake up and remember what you've lost. Maybe it was a beloved family member, a close friend, or even a dream that slipped through your fingers. Maybe your marriage ended, or someone you trusted deeply betrayed you. Grief can come in so many forms, and each one carries a sting that's unique and personal. When our hearts are broken, it can feel like we're walking through a long, dark tunnel with no exit in sight. Yet Jesus Christ and our Heavenly Father know exactly what we're going through. The question is, how do we open ourselves to the healing They offer?

The scriptures repeatedly describe the Savior as the One who binds up the brokenhearted (Psalm 147:3, KJV). That's not just poetic language—it's a promise. When Jesus read in the synagogue, He specifically quoted Isaiah, saying He was sent "to heal the brokenhearted" (Luke 4:18, KJV). That mission is deeply personal. Our tears, sleepless nights, and moments of despair matter to Him. Think about how He wept at the tomb of Lazarus, even though He knew He was about to raise him from the dead (John 11:35, KJV). Why would Jesus weep if He had the power to fix it instantly? Perhaps because He empathized with the raw, crushing sorrow of those around Him, and He wanted them—and us—to know He cares about our pain in a very real, human way.

Grief can be complicated. Sometimes, we're hit by multiple losses all at once, leaving us spinning. Other times, we think we're past the worst of it, and then a memory or an anniversary date plunges us right back into sorrow. That's normal. Healing is rarely a straight line. If you've lost a loved one to death, you might wonder how you're ever going to fill that empty chair at the dinner table or quiet the ache that comes in waves at unexpected moments. If you've gone through a divorce, you might still be grieving the future you imagined. If you've faced any kind of shattered expectation, you might be questioning God's plan or even your own worth. Let me gently remind you that these emotional roller coasters don't scare the Lord. He walks with you in every loop and twist.

One reason heartbreak can be so debilitating is that it often shakes our identity. We tie our sense of self to certain relationships or roles, and when they crumble, we feel like we crumble too. But the gospel reminds us that our truest identity is as children of Heavenly Father—beloved, eternal souls who can never lose that divine heritage, no matter what changes here on earth. Romans 8:16–17 says we are children of God, "and if children, then heirs" (KJV). That heritage doesn't vanish if someone walks out of our life or if mortality claims a loved one. We remain anchored in God's family, with a destiny that extends beyond this life's heartbreak.

Still, knowing that in our minds doesn't always console our hearts right away. That's where the Savior's invitation to "come unto me, all ye that labour and are heavy laden" takes on personal meaning (Matthew 11:28, KJV). Coming unto Christ with our heartbreak means being vulnerable in prayer. Instead of a quick "thank you for my blessings," it might look like, "Heavenly Father, I'm broken. I feel abandoned, scared, and hopeless. Please help me make it through today." Honest prayer often becomes the channel through which divine comfort can flow, and while it might not erase our pain instantly, it can bring moments of calm and reassurance that God sees our tears.

If you're grieving the death of a loved one, the doctrine of the Resurrection can be a life raft. In the Book of Mormon, we read that Christ "breaketh the bands of death" (Mosiah 15:8), making it possible for all of us to rise again. This isn't just a hopeful fairy tale; it's the core of the Christian message—Jesus rose from the dead so we could too (1 Corinthians 15:20–22, KJV). The separation we feel from those who've passed is real, but it's temporary. We can be reunited, and those glorious reunions will make our current sorrow feel like a "small moment" in comparison (Doctrine and Covenants 121:7, 2013). Does that mean we shouldn't mourn? Not at all. Mourning is part of love. But we can mourn with hope, knowing death doesn't have the final say.

For those grieving a lost relationship or a shattered dream, the principle is similar: God's plan is bigger than our heartbreak. He can open new doors, craft new paths, and bring beauty from ashes (Isaiah 61:3, KJV). That doesn't mean we gloss over our pain or rush ourselves to "just move on." Healing takes time, and it's often a step-by-step process where we learn deeper trust in the Lord. At times, we might feel like the shattered pieces of our life can't possibly be put back together. But we worship a Savior who specializes in restoration. Elder Jeffrey R. Holland reassured us that "no one is so far gone that they cannot be rescued" (Holland, 2009, p. 87).

If He can rescue our souls from sin, He can also mend our hearts from sorrow.

Sometimes, heartbreak is accompanied by guilt, especially if we feel partially responsible for what happened. Maybe there were harsh words we wish we could take back, or choices we regret that contributed to a falling-out. The Savior's Atonement covers not only sins but also the anguish of regret. Alma 7:11–12 (Book of Mormon) explains that Jesus took upon Himself all our pains so that He would know how to comfort us. That includes the pain of wishing we had done things differently. We can humbly confess our part in the situation, seek forgiveness where needed (both from God and from others), and then allow ourselves to be cleansed of shame. The Savior doesn't want us to live in perpetual self-flagellation; He wants us to learn, grow, and move forward. That's part of the healing process.

Seeking help from others can also be crucial. Heartbreak can isolate us if we let it, convincing us that no one cares or understands. But leaning on trusted friends, family members, church leaders, or even professional counselors can bring fresh perspectives and comfort. Sometimes we just need a safe space to cry, vent, or process our thoughts. Galatians 6:2 tells us to "bear one another's burdens" (KJV), and heartbreak is certainly a burden we shouldn't have to carry alone. Reaching out doesn't indicate weakness; it's an act of courage and faith, showing God we're willing to accept the help He might provide through His earthly angels.

One tender way God can bring healing is through the gentle nudge of the Holy Spirit at unexpected times. You might be driving or folding laundry, and suddenly a memory of a loved one pops into your mind—but instead of crushing grief, you feel a peaceful warmth. That's no coincidence. It can be a spiritual reassurance that our relationships aren't lost forever, that God is aware of our sadness, and that He's quietly whispering hope. President Russell M. Nelson taught that "the Lord loves effort, and effort brings rewards" (Nelson, 2020, p. 82). As we make the effort to keep our hearts open to the Spirit—even in our pain—we create space for these tender mercies to sink in and soothe us.

We also need to have patience with ourselves. If someone says, "Just get over it," they probably don't grasp the magnitude of your loss. Heartbreak doesn't adhere to a neat timeline. Even the Savior, who is perfect, chose to mourn Lazarus before raising him (John 11:34–35, KJV). That tells me that taking time to grieve is not a lack of faith; it's part of being human. Sometimes, we worry that prolonged grief means we're spiritually weak, but that's not necessarily true. Elder Dale G. Renlund once noted that our spiritual growth can come "line upon line" (Renlund, 2015, p. 105). Emotional healing often follows a similar principle—it unfolds gradually, and we might go through phases of denial, anger, bargaining, depression, and acceptance. God's love is big enough to hold us through every stage.

At some point, we may begin to see that our suffering has enlarged our ability to empathize. When we encounter someone else going through a similar heartbreak, we suddenly understand them in a way we couldn't have before. That's part of the beauty of sorrow—it can refine our hearts, making them softer, more compassionate. As we comfort others with the comfort we've received from the Lord (2 Corinthians 1:4, KJV), we become conduits of His healing power. Our wounds, once raw and bleeding, can become sources of light and hope for others. That doesn't make the pain "worth it" in a simplistic sense, but it does mean God can bring profound meaning out of our darkest nights.

If your heartbreak involves waiting—maybe you're longing for a child, a marriage partner, a healing miracle, or some other blessing—patience in the

Lord's timing is part of the healing process. Psalm 27:14 counsels, "Wait on the Lord: be of good courage" (KJV). Waiting can be excruciating, especially when we see others receiving the very blessings we crave. But a broken heart combined with patience can create a fertile ground for miracles. The Book of Mormon includes countless accounts of individuals who waited on the Lord through pain and eventually received deliverance, though rarely on their expected timetable (Mosiah 24:10–16, for example). In hindsight, those waiting periods often proved critical in strengthening faith and forging deeper humility.

For those who have lost hope altogether—perhaps you've prayed and prayed, yet your heartbreak persists—remember that Jesus Himself experienced a moment of profound anguish when He asked if the cup could pass from Him (Matthew 26:39, KJV). Though His Father didn't remove that cup, an angel was sent to strengthen Him (Luke 22:43, KJV). Sometimes, God's answer isn't to erase our trial but to give us the spiritual resources to endure it. In that endurance, we can discover a closeness with Him that transcends what we might have known otherwise. Elder Neal A. Maxwell poignantly said, "The very act of choosing to be a disciple can bring to us a certain special suffering" (Maxwell, 1997, p. 96). But that suffering, when consecrated to the Lord, can become sanctifying.

Another piece of healing is learning to forgive—even if the heartbreak wasn't your fault. Forgiveness doesn't excuse wrongdoing, but it does free us from the chains of bitterness that can keep our wounds from healing. The Savior, in His final hours, prayed, "Father, forgive them; for they know not what they do" (Luke 23:34, KJV). That's our ultimate example. Forgiving someone who caused our heartbreak can feel impossible on our own, but with the enabling power of the Atonement, we can gradually release the anger and pain that poison our hearts. That doesn't mean we instantly trust the person again or allow unsafe situations. It means we place our burdens at the Savior's feet, letting Him carry the weight of judgment while we move forward toward wholeness.

Healing also involves a measure of self-compassion. Heartbreak can leave us blaming ourselves for not being strong enough, smart enough, or faithful enough to prevent what happened. But the reality is that life throws us challenges we can't always control. The Savior doesn't stand over us with a clipboard, tallying our failures to handle pain gracefully. He beckons us with outstretched arms. When we approach Him with humility, we don't have to have it all together. He meets us right where we are, offering grace for our weaknesses and comfort for our sorrows.

I've known people who felt their heartbreak would never end. Some lost children, some battled chronic illnesses, others faced devastating betrayals. Over time—sometimes a long time—they found that the Savior's love had walked with them each step of the way, gently turning despair into a tender hope. They still carry scars, but those scars became reminders of a deep, personal relationship with Jesus Christ, rather than permanent badges of defeat. That's the miracle of the gospel: Christ transforms our darkest chapters into testimony-building experiences if we trust Him enough to keep going.

It might help to create simple rituals of remembrance and hope. Some people write letters to their departed loved one, or they keep a journal of thoughts and prayers during their grief. Others mark certain anniversaries with a small act of service, turning a day of sorrow into a day of kindness. These practices can keep us connected to the reality that heartbreak, while painful, is not the end of our story. We can acknowledge our loss while affirming that we still have a future with God, a future that can hold joy again.

Above all, I hope you remember this: heartbreak doesn't mean you're unworthy of love or success. It means you've loved deeply or yearned sincerely, and something precious was taken from you. That's part of mortality. But Jesus Christ descended below all things (Doctrine and Covenants 88:6) so that He could lift us above them. No matter how broken you feel, He can piece you back together. No matter how big the void in your life, He can fill it with His grace. No matter how hopeless your nights, He can bring dawn. And when you finally come out on the other side of your grief—maybe in this life, maybe in the next—you'll carry a deeper empathy, a stronger faith, and a greater assurance that your Savior truly knows you.

If you take nothing else from this chapter, please take this: it's okay to grieve. It's okay to be sad, angry, or confused for a while. But invite Jesus Christ into that sadness. Let Him sit with you, cry with you, and slowly mend your heart. Let Heavenly Father whisper His love to you in small, quiet moments. And as you do, day by day, you'll feel glimmers of light returning. You'll realize you're stronger than you thought, not because of your own power, but because the power of God is real and active in your life. Healing is a process, but it's a sacred one. Your tears are known to the God who made you, and He will not abandon you now.

Chapter 8: Trusting God Through Hard Times

I think we'd all agree there are days when life feels like one giant obstacle course. You zigzag through one crisis, only to find another one waiting around the corner. It can be tough, bewildering, and sometimes downright discouraging. When the financial rug slips out from under you, or when a relationship turns sour, or when your best efforts still don't yield the desired outcome, it's natural to wonder where God is in all this. Is He watching? Does He care? If you've ever had those questions—and let's face it, most of us have—then this chapter is for you. We're going to talk about trusting God through hard times, even when your world seems shaky.

Let me start by offering a bit of hope: Hard times don't mean God has abandoned you. In fact, scripturally speaking, it's often during challenging seasons that He's working the most tenderly in your life. We see this pattern in both the Bible and the Book of Mormon. If you think about Job—he lost almost everything. Yet somehow, in the midst of his unimaginable trials, Job managed to declare, "Though he slay me, yet will I trust in him"

(Job 13:15, King James Version). He had this extraordinary faith that even in his darkest hour, God was still God—still worthy of trust, still intimately involved in his journey. That doesn't mean Job never felt pain or confusion. But it does show us that a bedrock trust in Heavenly Father can remain standing even when storms rage.

We sometimes assume that if God really loves us, He'll shield us from trouble. Yet Jesus told His disciples, "In the world ye shall have tribulation" (John 16:33, KJV). He didn't say we might have tribulation—He said we shall. That's as certain as it gets. But notice how that verse ends: "But be of good cheer; I have overcome the world." That's a powerful statement. The Savior acknowledges that hardship is inevitable, but He reminds us that He has power over every kind of trouble life can throw at us. Hard times don't catch Him off guard. And when we trust Him, we're essentially hitching our wagon to the One who's already conquered sin, sorrow, and even death.

Still, trusting Him can be tricky when life unravels. Financial strain, heartbreak, illness, or any number of personal crises can make us question whether God really has our back. One thing that helps is to remember that Heavenly Father sees the entire tapestry of our lives, whereas we only see a handful of threads at a time. From our limited vantage point, a painful event might look pointless. But from His eternal perspective, it could be an instrumental piece in our growth, shaping us into the people He knows we can become. Elder Neal A. Maxwell once described trials as "tempering processes" (Maxwell, 1974, p. 12)—the spiritual equivalent of forging steel. That's not to trivialize our pain, but it does hint at the possibility that these tests can refine us.

Trusting God doesn't mean putting on a fake smile and ignoring your feelings. It's okay to be honest with Him about your struggles. In fact, that honesty can deepen your relationship with Him. Look at the Psalms—over and over, we see raw prayers of lament. King David cries out in desperation, and at times you can almost hear him say, "Lord, where are You?" (Psalm 10:1, KJV). But David's prayers usually circle back to a reaffirmation of faith: "Thou hast been my defence and refuge in the day of my trouble" (Psalm 59:16, KJV). Acknowledging your worries doesn't negate your trust; it can actually strengthen it. Because when you pour out your heart and then choose to believe God's promises anyway, that's faith in action.

Sometimes, we need to break down trust into practical steps. First, pray honestly. Don't hold back your fears or doubts. If you feel like you've done everything right and still face roadblocks, tell Him that. Invite His guidance, His comfort, and yes, even His correction if there's something you need to learn. The second step is to seek revelation. The Lord may not always give you a direct answer, but He can provide peace, direction, or a sense of reassurance through the Holy Spirit. Many times, that peace comes as a gentle whisper that calms the turmoil in your heart. The third step is to act on whatever inspiration you receive. Faith isn't passive; it's meant to propel us forward. Even small steps in the direction you feel guided to take can show Heavenly Father that you're serious about trusting Him.

Another thing to remember is that God's timeline rarely aligns with ours. We live in a world where we want instant everything—instant gratification, instant results, instant relief. But God has an eternal view. Elder Dieter F. Uchtdorf once said, "Heavenly Father's love for you is so great that He cannot save you in your sins, but He will save you from your sins if you turn to Him" (Uchtdorf, 2007, p. 101). That statement focuses on sin, but the principle also applies to challenges: He might not spare us from every trial, but He will strengthen us through them when we lean on

Him. And that strengthening often takes time—time to grow in faith, time to develop patience, time to become more like Christ.

Perhaps you're dealing with a crisis so big you feel paralyzed. It could be the loss of a job, a betrayal in your marriage, a devastating illness, or something else that has flipped your world upside down. Let me assure you that there's no pit so deep that God's love isn't deeper still. The Savior knows the feeling of utter anguish—He sweat great drops of blood in Gethsemane (Luke 22:44, KJV). He understands suffering on a level we can't fully comprehend, and that's why He can stand by you in yours. Alma 7:11 (Book of Mormon) teaches that He took upon Himself not just sins, but also pains, infirmities, and afflictions—meaning He walked through the valley of every heartbreak so He could lead us out of it.

Often, our ability to trust God grows when we reflect on how He's helped us in the past. Think back: has there been a time when a solution appeared just when you needed it? A time when a friend or family member stepped in with the exact kind of support you were praying for? Or perhaps a moment when you felt a wave of peace that surpassed logical understanding? Those experiences, however small, serve as spiritual markers. They remind us that God hasn't failed us before—and if He's the same yesterday, today, and forever (Hebrews 13:8, KJV), then He won't fail us now. Reflecting on past blessings builds our confidence in present trials.

If you're someone who likes to fix problems on your own, trusting God can feel uncomfortable, almost like surrendering control. But the truth is, control is often an illusion. We can do our best, but life has a way of throwing variables at us that we can't predict or manage. Trusting God doesn't mean we stop doing everything in our power. It means we acknowledge that our power alone isn't enough—and that's where the divine partnership begins. King Benjamin said, "Ye must press forward with a steadfastness in Christ" (Mosiah 3:19, Book of Mormon). Being steadfast in Christ is about doing all we can while recognizing that He is the one who ultimately holds the keys to our success and peace.

Another reason trust falters is because we worry that if we fully trust God, He might lead us somewhere we don't want to go or ask us to do something uncomfortable. The rich young ruler in the New Testament was willing to follow Jesus—up to a point (Matthew 19:16–22, KJV). When Jesus asked him to give up his possessions, the young man went away sorrowful, because that cost was too high. Sometimes we're afraid God might ask us to let go of a dream, a habit, or even a relationship that isn't good for us. But remember, anything He asks us to do ultimately leads to growth and greater happiness, even if we can't see it in the moment. He doesn't delight in our pain—He delights in our eternal well-being. If He's guiding you to make a change or step into the unknown, trust that He sees a horizon you can't yet imagine.

Let's talk about the role of community. Trying to trust God in isolation can be doubly hard. When we gather with fellow believers or talk with trusted friends about our struggles, we often find encouragement that bolsters our faith. Hearing someone else's story of how the Lord came through for them can be just what we need in our darkest hour. That's why testimonies matter. Revelation 12:11 says we "overcame him by the blood of the Lamb, and by the word of their testimony" (KJV). Sharing our experiences, or even listening to others, can spark renewed trust in the God who is no respecter of persons (Acts 10:34, KJV)—if He helped them, He'll help us.

Now, what if you're in a place where you've prayed for deliverance, but it hasn't come yet? That might be the hardest test of all. The

Book of Mormon gives an example in the people of Alma, who were in bondage under a cruel ruler. They prayed for deliverance, but initially, the burden didn't vanish. Instead, the Lord strengthened them so the burdens felt lighter (Mosiah 24:14–15, Book of Mormon). Only later did He miraculously free them. That pattern is instructive. Sometimes God's first step isn't to remove the trial but to make us stronger in it. If you find yourself still waiting for that big breakthrough, watch for the smaller mercies—maybe you sense an inexplicable calm, or maybe you discover a hidden reservoir of resilience you never knew you had.

Another aspect of trusting God is trusting in His justice. We live in a world where cruelty, dishonesty, and injustice can seem to prosper while good people suffer. If you've been on the receiving end of unfairness, you might wonder why God allows it. It can help to remember that this life isn't the final chapter of the story. There is a day of reckoning when all wrongs will be made right (Revelation 20:12, KJV). That doesn't erase the pain we feel here and now, but it does mean we don't have to carry the burden of exacting justice ourselves. The Lord says, "Vengeance is mine; I will repay" (Romans 12:19, KJV). That assurance can free us to focus on our own growth and healing, rather than stewing in anger or bitterness.

When the storm rages hardest, sometimes the best we can do is anchor ourselves in the simplest truths: God is good. Jesus is the Savior. We are known and loved by our Heavenly Father. We have a divine destiny. These truths might feel like flickering candles in a hurricane, but they're actually unshakeable when we hold fast to them. President Russell M. Nelson taught that "the joy we feel has little to do with the circumstances of our lives and everything to do with the focus of our lives" (Nelson, 2016, p. 80). If our focus is on trusting God, we can find moments of joy even when circumstances are far from ideal.

It's also worth noting that trusting God doesn't mean we shouldn't plan, prepare, or take practical steps. If you're facing financial trouble, for example, trusting God can include making a budget, seeking employment opportunities, or getting professional advice. Faith and works go hand in hand (James 2:17, KJV). The difference is that we do our part without letting panic or despair rule us. Instead of spiraling into worst-case scenarios, we invite the Lord to guide our decisions and multiply our efforts. When we do, we often find that He opens doors we didn't see coming.

You might also consider journaling your experiences. Writing down the times you've felt God's presence or guidance can serve as a powerful reminder when new storms arise. Sometimes, rereading those entries can rekindle your trust when it's grown dim. Elder Henry B. Eyring shared how he used to write in his journal daily, focusing on how he saw "the hand of the Lord" in his life (Eyring, 2007, p. 70). Over time, this practice helped him recognize that God was always involved, even in small ways. You might try something similar, noting not just the big miracles, but the subtle nudges and impressions that have kept you moving forward.

As you continue to trust God, expect moments when doubt creeps in. That's part of the mortal experience. The adversary would love to convince you that your troubles mean God isn't real, or that if He is real, He doesn't care. But the enemy's arguments fall flat when we stand on the bedrock of personal witness. Even if all you have is a mustard seed of faith (Matthew 17:20, KJV), cling to it. Talk to your Heavenly Father about your doubts. Ask Him to strengthen your faith. Sometimes, the reassurance you need comes not from external evidence, but from the quiet confirmation of the Spirit that whispers, "He's with you. Keep going."

Eventually, many of our trials pass—or at least change form—and we look back amazed at how we made it through. We realize that even though we didn't see it at the time, God was orchestrating events or sending people into our lives at just the right moments. That hindsight can bolster our faith for the next set of challenges. We begin to say, "If He helped me then, He'll help me now." It's an ongoing relationship of trust, each chapter of our lives adding another layer of testimony that God's promises are sure.

Wherever you are on your path—whether you're in the middle of a crisis or just now catching your breath from one—I invite you to test these principles. Open your heart to the possibility that God is more involved than you think, that His love is deeper than you've imagined, and that the Savior's Atonement really does extend to every form of suffering. Trusting God through hard times isn't an easy, one-and-done exercise. It's more like a daily choice to believe that, despite appearances, you're not alone. And as you make that choice day after day, you'll gradually sense His hand upholding you, giving you courage to face whatever comes. The storm may still rage, but you'll feel a peace that doesn't depend on external circumstances—a peace rooted in the reality that your Heavenly Father is in control, and He will see you safely through.

Chapter 9: The Power of Forgiveness

If there's one principle that can lighten our hearts and mend countless wounds, it's forgiveness. Yet forgiveness can also feel like the hardest thing in the world, especially when someone has hurt us deeply. We struggle with questions like, "Why should I let go of my anger when they haven't even apologized?" or "Won't forgiveness mean I'm condoning what they did?" These are valid concerns. But scripture makes it clear: "If ye forgive men their trespasses, your heavenly Father will also forgive you" (Matthew 6:14, KJV). That's a strong statement, and it underscores that forgiveness isn't just a suggestion—it's central to the gospel of Jesus Christ.

Sometimes, we associate forgiveness with a single act: we say the words "I forgive you" and think that's it. But genuine forgiveness is often a process—sometimes a long, winding one. It can involve repeated decisions to release resentment, especially if the hurt comes to mind over and over. Elder Neil L. Andersen described forgiveness as "a deep, personal decision, an act of faith in the Lord" (Andersen, 2007, p. 86). That means it's not about waiting for perfect circumstances; it's about choosing to trust God's command and God's promises.

Let's start by clearing up a common misconception: Forgiveness does not mean excusing wrongdoing or pretending it never happened. God Himself, who is the epitome of forgiveness, still acknowledges sin as sin. He doesn't sweep it under the rug; He offers us a path to repent and be cleansed. Similarly, when we forgive someone, we don't have to say, "It was no big deal." Sometimes, it was a very big deal. What we're doing is relinquishing the emotional shackles that keep us bound to the offense. We're saying, "I refuse to let this hurt poison my life any longer."

One reason forgiveness is so crucial is that it breaks the cycle of bitterness. When we cling to anger or resentment, it can fester and grow, affecting our mood, our relationships, and even our physical health. We might think our anger punishes the offender, but more often it punishes us. There's a quote that says, "Holding a grudge is like drinking poison and expecting the other person to die." Whether we attribute that to various sources, the sentiment rings true. Bitterness rarely harms the one who wronged us; it mainly harms the one clinging to it.

For many of us, the sticking point is that forgiving can feel like surrendering a sense of justice. We want the other person to pay for what they did. But the scriptures remind us: "Vengeance is mine; I will repay, saith the Lord" (Romans 12:19, KJV). This doesn't mean God delights in punishing people. It means He's the only one qualified to judge perfectly. He knows every intention of the heart, every mitigating circumstance, and every step someone takes toward repentance. When we insist on carrying the burden of vengeance ourselves, we're taking a role that belongs to God alone. Trusting Him with ultimate justice frees us to move on.

Jesus provided the ultimate example of forgiveness on the cross. In the midst of unimaginable pain, He prayed, "Father, forgive them; for they know not what they do" (Luke 23:34, KJV). That short sentence encapsulates a universe of compassion. He recognized that the very people driving nails into His hands were blinded by ignorance and hardened hearts. We can draw strength from that example. If the sinless Son of God can offer forgiveness while suffering so intensely, perhaps we can muster the courage to forgive those who've wounded us—though, admittedly, it might not come in a single instant.

It might help to break the process down. First, acknowledge the hurt. Don't minimize it or cover it up. Being truthful about your pain is part of emotional honesty. Second, take that hurt to Heavenly Father in prayer. Pour out your feelings, your anger, your longing for justice. Third, ask for the desire to forgive—even if you're not there yet. Sometimes, you have to pray for the willingness to begin the journey. Fourth, remember that the power to forgive ultimately comes from Christ's Atonement, not from sheer willpower. Alma 7:11–12 (Book of Mormon) tells us Christ took upon Himself our pains and afflictions so He can know how to succor us. That includes the pain of being wronged and the uphill battle of letting go. He stands ready to share His enabling grace.

Some situations involve deep trauma—abuse, betrayal, or ongoing harm. Forgiveness does not require us to stay in a dangerous situation or ignore wise boundaries. If someone has abused you, you can still forgive while seeking protection or legal recourse if necessary. Forgiveness is about releasing hatred and bitterness, not about forfeiting safety. The Savior, who confronted evil head-on, certainly does not expect us to be doormats for repeated harm. Rather, He invites us to let go of malice and trust Him to deal with the person's accountability. This distinction is critical—sometimes people confuse forgiveness with passivity, but in reality, you can forgive and still say "enough" to ongoing mistreatment.

We also need to talk about self-forgiveness, which can be every bit as challenging as forgiving others. Many of us carry guilt for mistakes and sins, long after we've confessed and tried to make things right. We replay our failures, telling ourselves we're hopeless or irredeemable. The adversary loves that—if he can keep us mired in shame, we won't fully embrace the liberating power of Christ's grace. But 2 Nephi 2:8 (Book of Mormon) reminds us that the Savior's Atonement is infinite. If He declares us forgiven upon sincere repentance, who are we to argue? Holding onto guilt after God has let it go suggests we think our judgment is higher than His. It's humbling to admit that He's more merciful than we sometimes are to ourselves.

One tool for forgiveness—both of others and self—is remembering our own need for mercy. Jesus taught the parable of the unmerciful servant (Matthew 18:23–35, KJV). This servant owed a massive debt but was forgiven by his master. Then he went out and refused to forgive a tiny debt owed to him by someone else. The master was furious when he heard about it. The lesson? We can't expect unlimited forgiveness from God if we refuse to extend it to others. That doesn't mean we rush the process, but it does remind us that we're all in need of grace. Elder Jeffrey R. Holland once said, "We must extend to each other the grace and forgiveness we so earnestly desire for ourselves" (Holland, 2012, p. 31). That hits home, doesn't it?

Yet, the path to real forgiveness can feel like it has more switchbacks than a mountain trail. We might genuinely forgive one day, only to feel the hurt flare up again when triggered by a memory or a fresh offense. Don't despair if that happens—it's normal. Simply reaffirm your decision to forgive, pray for help again, and keep walking forward. Over time, those flare-ups become less frequent and less intense. President Russell M. Nelson taught that "through the power of the Atonement of Jesus Christ, all of life's inequalities will be made right" (Nelson, 2013, p. 94). Holding onto that hope can keep us going when the journey feels long.

Another aspect is learning to see the person who hurt us the way God sees them. This doesn't excuse their behavior, but it can soften our anger. We're all children of Heavenly Father, and sometimes people act out of ignorance, fear, or their own woundedness. Again, that doesn't justify the harm they caused, but it can remind us that they, too, are in desperate need of the Savior's healing. Sometimes, as we pray for someone who's hurt us—really pray that they'll find repentance, peace, and blessings—our heart shifts. That shift doesn't automatically erase the consequences of their actions, but it can make it easier to release resentment. The more we see each other as beloved souls in progress, the easier it becomes to choose compassion over retaliation.

Forgiveness also liberates us from being defined by our wounds. When we hold onto grudges, we let the offense occupy a central place in our identity. But we are so much more than the sum of what happened to us. We have divine potential and eternal worth that nothing can erase. By forgiving, we step out of the victim role and into the role of a healed, growing disciple of Christ. We reclaim our ability to move forward unburdened. That's not an overnight transformation, but every small decision to forgive chips away at the chains tying us to the past.

In some cases, you might never reconcile with the person you forgave—maybe the relationship is beyond repair or it's simply not safe to reopen that door. Forgiveness and reconciliation are not always the same. Reconciliation requires mutual effort and willingness to heal the relationship. Forgiveness, on the other hand, is a personal, one-sided act of letting go. It's primarily between you and God, even though it's about someone else's actions. If reconciliation is possible, wonderful. If not, you can still free your heart by forgiving.

Let's circle back to the Savior's role, because He's the linchpin of true forgiveness. Without His Atonement, we'd be stuck with our sins, and we'd have no divine empowerment to release resentment. With it, we have a path to be cleansed, to receive comfort, and to tap into a reservoir of love that transcends mortal limits. Think about how the Savior looked at those who crucified Him. He understood their ignorance, and He loved them despite their horrific actions. When we pray to emulate that love, we're not just wishing upon a star. We're asking to participate in Christ's divine capacity to love beyond reason. And while we might never reach that level perfectly in this life, every step in that direction brings greater peace.

Forgiveness can also be an act of faith in Heavenly Father's plan of happiness. We trust that He can bring good out of our painful experiences. That doesn't mean He willed those experiences, especially if they resulted from someone's misuse of agency. But it does mean He can help us grow through adversity, become more empathetic, and even transform our wounds into spiritual gifts that enable us to comfort others. Romans 8:28 promises that "all things work together for good to them that love God" (KJV). Forgiveness is one way we show that we love and trust Him enough to let Him handle the final accounting of justice and mercy.

Sometimes, the hardest person to forgive is ourselves, especially if we think we've messed up irreparably. But the Savior's grace is greater than any mistake. The path of repentance might be painful, requiring humility, restitution, and real change. Yet the end result is liberation. Don't let shame tell you you're unworthy of forgiveness. That's like telling the sun it can't shine on you. The sun just shines; it's in its nature. Similarly, Christ's love and forgiveness are always there, waiting for us to accept them. The question is whether we'll let go of our guilt and actually reach out for His outstretched hand.

As we strive to forgive, we can do practical things to reinforce our choice. We can study scriptures on mercy, love, and compassion. We can fill our minds with uplifting music or talks that remind us of our divine heritage. We can visualize ourselves handing our hurts to the Savior and walking away lighter. We can also serve others—sometimes focusing on blessing someone else's life takes our mind off the cycle of resentment. Elder Dale G. Renlund said, "As we develop greater faith in Jesus Christ, we must… treat the children of God with greater kindness" (Renlund, 2016, p. 98). That includes ourselves and those who hurt us.

Expect setbacks. Forgiveness rarely happens in a straight line. You might think you've finally let go, only to find the bitterness reemerging. Keep turning to the Lord. Keep praying for His grace. Sometimes a single hurt can reappear many times before it finally loses its hold on your heart. That's normal. Each time you choose forgiveness again, you're strengthening your spiritual muscles, just like a workout that gradually builds endurance.

Ultimately, forgiveness aligns us with the heart of God. John 3:16 says, "For God so loved the world, that he gave his only begotten Son…" (KJV). If God can love a fallen world enough to offer His Son, can't we strive to love each other a fraction of that amount by letting go of hatred? It's a tall order, but it's central to becoming Christlike. And the result is freedom—freedom from the cage of anger, freedom to heal, freedom to move forward with hope instead of being anchored in the past.

It may help to remember that extending forgiveness can plant seeds of change in others. Our willingness to forgive might soften a hardened heart or inspire someone to seek God's grace for themselves. We don't forgive just for that reason, but it's a wonderful possible outcome. Even if it doesn't happen, we've obeyed the Lord's command and secured our own peace. That alone is a miracle worth celebrating.

So wherever you are on the forgiveness spectrum—maybe you're just starting to thaw your anger, or maybe you've been working on forgiving for years—know that Heavenly Father honors your efforts. He doesn't expect instant perfection, but He does invite you to keep trying, keep praying, and keep trusting. The power of forgiveness is real. It can mend relationships, heal deep wounds, and bring us closer to the Savior's own heart. In a world often fueled by outrage, what a relief it is to know that through Christ, we can choose a different path—a path of compassion, mercy, and ultimately, love.

Chapter 10: Rising Above Shame

I'd like to start by painting a picture in your mind. Imagine you're walking down a long hallway, and on both sides are doors labeled with all the negative things you've ever believed about yourself: "Not Good Enough," "Damaged," "Unworthy," "Unlovable," "Failure," and so on. As you keep walking, you notice those doors are wide open, beckoning you to step in and settle under the weight of shame. That's what shame does—it tries to lock us into rooms labeled with lies about our identity and worth. It tells us that because we made a mistake, we are a mistake. Or because something painful happened to us, we're irreparably broken. If you're carrying that kind of shame, this chapter is for you.

Let's start by clarifying the difference between shame and guilt. Guilt says, "I did something wrong; I need to make it right." In a healthy way, guilt can motivate us to repent and learn. Shame, on the other hand, says, "I am something wrong; there's no hope for me." While guilt can be productive, shame paralyzes us, robbing us of the belief that we can change or that Christ's Atonement applies to us. Elder Jeffrey R. Holland once said that shame often masquerades as humility, but it's actually "destructive and counterfeit" (Holland, 2013, p. 88). True humility invites us to rely on the Savior; shame tells us we're beyond His reach.

But here's the gospel truth: no one is beyond the Savior's reach. Isaiah 1:18 famously declares, "Though your sins be as scarlet, they shall be as white as snow" (King James Version). That's a promise directed to all of us, no exceptions. If you find yourself hesitant to approach God because you feel unworthy or tainted, I want to remind you of something important: Heavenly Father already knows everything about you. Every mistake, every secret, every regret—and He still loves you fiercely. Jesus Christ didn't atone for a select group; He atoned for the whole world, including those who feel deeply ashamed.

Often, shame whispers that our worth is tied to our performance. If we haven't lived up to a certain standard—be it spiritual, moral, academic, or otherwise—we might conclude we're "less than." But the scriptures teach a different perspective: our worth is inherent as children of God. We didn't earn it, so we can't lose it. Yes, our choices matter, and yes, we're accountable for them. But our divine worth remains constant. President Russell M. Nelson taught that "your individual worth... is absolute. Your potential is limitless" (Nelson, 1990, p. 85). Think about that. If your worth is absolute, shame's attempt to brand you as worthless has no standing in eternal truth.

Shame can also creep in from experiences where we didn't necessarily sin, but were sinned against or hurt by others. Sometimes abuse survivors feel shame, as though they were responsible for what happened. That's a cruel trick of the adversary. If that's your situation, please know that no wrongdoing done to you can stain your intrinsic worth. Heavenly

Father sees past the hurt and confusion, and He recognizes that you are not defined by another person's actions. The Savior's Atonement covers the damage inflicted on us by others, too. Alma 7:11–12 (Book of Mormon) reminds us that Christ took upon Himself "pains and afflictions and temptations of every kind," so He could "know according to the flesh how to succor his people." That includes the unique torment of undeserved shame. He can empathize perfectly.

But how do we actually rise above shame when it feels so heavy? One step is recognizing it for what it is: a distortion. Shame twists truths about accountability and repentance, turning them into condemnation. We break that distortion by immersing ourselves in the Word of God. As we read scriptures, we discover stories of flawed people who were still beloved by the Lord. The apostle Paul persecuted the early Christians before his miraculous conversion (Acts 9, KJV). Alma the Younger fought against the church prior to his change of heart (Mosiah 27, Book of Mormon). Each of these individuals could have wallowed in shame, believing they were irredeemable. Yet God had a different plan for them—a plan of transformation and service. The same goes for us. He never sees us as "lost causes."

Another powerful tool against shame is prayer—honest, gut-level prayer. Sometimes we avoid prayer because shame tells us God is disappointed or even disgusted. In reality, that's the moment we need prayer most. When we openly confess our feelings to Heavenly Father—saying something like, "I'm drowning in shame; I feel completely unworthy, and I need Your help"—we crack open a door for divine grace to flow in. The Holy Spirit can gently whisper truths to our hearts, reminding us that we're loved, that repentance is possible, and that the Atonement is bigger than our mistakes.

We might not feel an instant wave of relief, but each honest prayer plants seeds of light in the darkness of shame.

It also helps to talk to someone you trust—maybe a close friend, a family member, or a church leader. Shame thrives in secrecy. When we stay silent, we feed the lie that we're alone in our unworthiness. But confiding in someone who truly cares can bring a sense of relief and perspective. They can reassure us that we're not monstrous or hopeless. They can also encourage us in practical ways, like seeking additional help if needed. Elder Dieter F. Uchtdorf once said, "We need to see ourselves as Heavenly Father sees us" (Uchtdorf, 2010, p. 87). Sometimes another person's compassionate perspective can help us glimpse that divine vision more clearly.

Now, let's address the question: If we've genuinely sinned, isn't shame appropriate? Isn't it good to feel bad about what we did? We need to differentiate between "godly sorrow" and destructive shame (see 2 Corinthians 7:10, KJV). Godly sorrow is a regret for sin that leads us to change our behavior and seek forgiveness. Destructive shame is a fixation on our "brokenness" that leads us to despair and turn away from God. The first draws us closer to the Savior; the second drives us farther from Him. Yes, it's healthy to feel remorse when we mess up. But the moment we start believing we can't be forgiven—that's shame talking, not the Spirit of God.

Healing from shame, especially if it's long-standing, might require time and patience. Maybe you've carried negative labels since childhood, or you've been told by others—family, peers, or even misguided religious leaders—that you're not measuring up. Replacing those old tapes with divine truth often involves daily efforts. Keep going back to scriptures and prayer. Memorize uplifting verses that remind you of Christ's love, such as

John 3:16 or Moroni 10:32. Write down impressions you receive from the Holy Spirit about your worth. Over time, these small actions can rewire your inner narrative, helping you see yourself through your Father's eyes.

Shame also shows up in perfectionism. We tell ourselves we must do everything flawlessly to be acceptable. But that's not the gospel either. Jesus didn't say, "Achieve perfection by Friday." He commanded us to "be ye therefore perfect" (Matthew 5:48, KJV), but in the context of learning to love as He loves—and we have an entire lifetime (and beyond) to grow into that. President Russell M. Nelson clarified that the word "perfect" in the scriptural context means "complete" or "finished" (Nelson, 1995, p. 48), suggesting a journey rather than an instantaneous state. We can strive for excellence without letting perfectionism trap us in a cycle of never feeling good enough.

It might also help to remember that you're not alone in battling shame. Many biblical and modern figures have wrestled with it, including Moses (Exodus 3:11, KJV) who questioned his ability, or Joseph Smith who faced enormous opposition and doubt (Joseph Smith—History 1:23, Pearl of Great Price). In each case, God reaffirmed His trust and love for these individuals, even as they felt inadequate. The same God stands ready to affirm you as well. No matter your age, background, or personal history, He's not tossing you aside. Shame might say you're disqualified from His grace, but He says, "My grace is sufficient for all men" (2 Nephi 25:23, Book of Mormon). That word all includes you.

If you've been stung by shame in a religious context—maybe you were told you'd never be forgiven or that your worth is conditional—please realize that such messages distort the essence of Christ's gospel. The Lord does set commandments and standards, but they're always accompanied by mercy, healing, and the invitation to come unto Him. The Book of

Mormon consistently preaches repentance as a hopeful act, a turning back to God who "will receive you" (Alma 5:33). That's the opposite of shame's message that you might as well give up.

One more tactic is to serve others. Shame often keeps us laser-focused on our perceived flaws. But when we shift our attention outward, we discover that we have something to offer. Maybe you're good at listening, cooking, writing letters, or fixing cars—whatever it is, using that skill to help someone can remind you that you're valuable to God's children. It doesn't mean you suddenly forget your struggles, but it does dilute shame's power. As you see the positive impact you can have, you begin to believe that you are indeed someone worthwhile, someone through whom the Lord can work good.

Realize, too, that Christ's Atonement didn't just erase sin—it also addresses the effects of sin, including shame. Elder Bruce C. Hafen likened the Atonement to both "paying the debt" and "fixing the car," meaning it covers more than forgiveness (Hafen, 2004, p. 34). The Savior can mend our broken hearts, lift our burdens, and show us how to see ourselves in a new light. You're not stuck in shame forever, no matter how long you've carried it. The path out might involve counseling, repentance, repeated reliance on prayer—but it's there, paved with the Savior's love.

At times, shame might seem like an old friend—familiar, even if it's destructive. Letting it go can feel unsettling, like stepping into unknown emotional territory. But stepping out of shame is worth it, because it aligns your self-concept with God's truth. President Boyd K. Packer once taught, "The study of the doctrines of the gospel will improve behavior quicker than a study of behavior will improve behavior" (Packer, 1977, p. 25). Why? Because the gospel tells us who we really are: children of a loving

Father, redeemed by a merciful Savior, destined for greater things. The more we internalize that, the more shame's hold loosens.

If you're reading this thinking, "I can't possibly shake off my past," let me share the comforting words of the Lord through the prophet Isaiah: "I have graven thee upon the palms of my hands" (Isaiah 49:16, KJV). The Savior literally bears marks that testify of His love and sacrifice for you. He can't forget you. And He doesn't want you hidden under layers of shame—He wants you free, standing in the light of His grace. Remember, the very meaning of the word "gospel" is "good news." And that good news applies to every single one of us, including you, no matter how weighed down by shame you feel.

The road ahead may involve ups and downs. Sometimes you might feel glimpses of freedom followed by old shame patterns flaring up again. Don't panic. Healing is often a process, not a single event. Keep turning to God's promises. Keep praying, keep studying, keep reaching out to loved ones or leaders who can bolster your confidence in Christ's power. And if you falter, that's okay—pick yourself back up and continue the journey. The Lord is patient, and He's infinitely more concerned about your continual progress than about momentary setbacks.

Shame would have you walk that hallway full of negative-labeled doors and step into one, never to leave. But you don't have to accept that invitation. With Christ's help, you can keep walking right past them, maybe even shutting them behind you. Instead, open the door labeled "Child of God." That's your true identity, and in that identity, shame has no permanent home. You were created for so much more than a life defined by mistakes or painful experiences. You were created to grow, to learn, to love, and ultimately to live with your Heavenly Father again—free of every lie that shame has tried to make you believe.

Chapter 11: Learning to Hear His Voice

Have you ever been in a crowded, noisy room, struggling to hear the voice of the person right next to you? That's sometimes how it feels when we're trying to hear the voice of God amidst the clamor of daily life. Between texts, social media, work obligations, and the general buzz of the world, it's easy to feel like we're missing out on divine direction. Yet, scripture after scripture reminds us that our Heavenly Father wants to communicate with us. If you've wondered how to tune in better to that still, small voice—how to recognize promptings from the Holy Ghost and feel that personal touch of revelation—then let's dive into what it means to truly "learn to hear His voice."

First, let's establish a simple but profound truth: God is not silent. He speaks through scriptures, prophets, personal revelation, and even the wonders of creation. Doctrine and Covenants 8:2 says He will "tell you in your mind and in your heart," indicating that revelation often comes through both our thoughts and our feelings (The Church of Jesus Christ of Latter-day Saints, 2013). But it's subtle. Think of Elijah's experience in 1 Kings 19:11–12, where God wasn't in the mighty wind, earthquake, or fire, but in "a still small voice" (KJV). That's often how the Spirit communicates—quietly, gently, and in a way we can easily miss if we're not paying attention.

One key to hearing His voice is creating space for it. In our fast-paced society, quiet moments can feel like a luxury we can't afford. But spiritual listening requires a measure of stillness. That could be five minutes of silent prayer in the morning before the rush of the day, or a late-night moment when the house is quiet. Even a short walk in nature, phone-free, can open a channel for the Spirit to speak. President Russell M. Nelson taught that, "Good inspiration is based upon good information" (Nelson, 2017, p. 39). We can't expect the Lord to talk over the noise we constantly invite in; we need to intentionally tune out distractions and tune in to Him.

Studying the scriptures is another key. When we immerse ourselves in God's written word, we become more familiar with the tone and content of His messages. The Holy Ghost can then highlight verses or phrases that speak directly to our current situation. I can't tell you how many times I've been reading a passage—one I've read before—and suddenly, something leaps off the page, applying perfectly to a question I've been wrestling with. That's no coincidence; that's revelation in action. Elder David A. Bednar taught that "most often, revelation comes in small increments over time and is granted according to our desire, worthiness, and preparation" (Bednar, 2011, p. 47). Scripture study is an act of preparation—it signals to the Lord that we're serious about hearing His counsel.

Prayer is, of course, the lifeblood of personal revelation. But how we pray matters. If we treat prayer like a checklist or a hurried monologue, we might not leave any space to listen. Consider finishing your prayers by pausing for a minute or two, asking, "Heavenly Father, is there anything You want me to learn or do?" and then just quietly waiting. We might feel an impression—a thought that seems to come from outside our normal stream of ideas. Or maybe a warm reassurance that we're on the right track. The Spirit's voice often feels like an internal nudge rather than an external sound. Over time, we learn to recognize that nudge more clearly.

Sometimes, we expect revelation to be dramatic—angels appearing, a voice echoing in the room. While that's certainly possible (and does happen scripturally), most of us will experience the Spirit in more subtle ways. President Boyd K. Packer described it as a "warmth, a glow" that provides certainty and peace (Packer, 1983, p. 66). That warmth may come during a sacrament meeting talk, a conversation with a friend, or even while doing everyday chores, if our hearts are open. The challenge is to resist the urge to dismiss those gentle feelings as just our own thoughts.

Another aspect of hearing God's voice is obedience. This might sound old-fashioned, but it's scriptural. John 7:17 teaches that if we do God's will, we will "know of the doctrine," meaning our spiritual understanding grows when we actually act on the light we've been given (KJV). Think about it: why would the Lord give us more direction if we haven't followed what He's already shared? Sometimes, we need to take the next right step—whatever prompting we've already received—before the Lord will unveil further guidance. Elder Richard G. Scott compared revelation to a puzzle, where we're often given just enough pieces to move forward in faith (Scott, 2009, p. 43).

But what if we're honestly trying to follow the Lord, and we still don't feel like we're hearing anything? We might wonder if we're just "spiritually tone-deaf." Rest assured, that's not the case. Some answers come as a "sunrise," gradually dawning on us over time (Bednar, 2011, p. 49). We might not notice the light changing until we look back and realize we're no longer in the dark. In the meantime, persist in prayer, scripture study, and doing good. God's silence isn't always a rejection—it can be a test of faith or a nudge to grow in patience. You're not alone in wondering why He sometimes delays His answers. The scriptures are filled with people who waited on the Lord—Abraham waited for a promised son, Hannah waited for a child, Joseph in Egypt waited years for deliverance. Each found that God's timetable, though mysterious, was perfect.

We also can't forget that we're all wired differently. Some people feel the Spirit powerfully through music, while others are touched more through intellectual study or quiet meditation. That's okay. There's no cookie-cutter formula for revelation. Elder Gary E. Stevenson said, "You don't have to be exactly like someone else... the Spirit will work with you in your own unique and individual ways" (Stevenson, 2017, p. 52). It helps to pay attention to situations where we've felt closest to God—maybe in nature, or during a temple visit, or while journaling—and then seek those opportunities more intentionally.

A common question is how to distinguish between our own thoughts and the voice of the Spirit. That's something we often learn through trial and error. Elder Dallin H. Oaks taught that "revelation is personal" and that we can gain confidence in recognizing it by acting on promptings and seeing the fruits (Oaks, 1981, p. 43). If you feel prompted to serve someone, do it. If you feel prompted to apologize, do it. Over time, you'll see how certain feelings lead to peace and confirmation, while others might lead nowhere. The Spirit's voice typically brings a sense of calm, clarity, or quiet confidence—even if it challenges us to step out of our comfort zone.

We also need to be aware that the adversary can mimic feelings of anxiety or discouragement, hoping we'll mistake them for revelation. The Lord's voice can be firm, but it's not cruel. Elder Ronald A. Rasband explained that "if a thought or feeling makes us anxious or fearful... it is not from the Lord" (Rasband, 2017, p. 95). That's not to say the Spirit can't warn us or jolt us out of complacency, but even warnings from God carry an undercurrent of love. They don't trap us in panic or shame; they guide us toward safety and repentance.

Let's address a scenario many of us face: we pray about a decision—what job to take, whether to move, whom to marry, and so forth—and we feel... nothing. It's tempting to think God is ignoring us. But sometimes He trusts us to use our agency. If you've studied your options, prayed for guidance, and don't feel a strong push in either direction, it might be a case where He's saying, "Choose for yourself, and I'll support you." That's not indifference; it's His confidence that you can make a good choice. Doctrine and Covenants 58:26–28 (LDS scripture) teaches that we shouldn't be "compelled in all things," but rather be "anxiously engaged" in doing good. In other words, sometimes God leaves the door open for us to decide, with the promise He'll help us flourish if our hearts are right.

Listening to the Spirit also involves a willingness to accept answers we don't expect. Sometimes we have our hearts set on a particular outcome, and we only want confirmation that yes, that's God's will. But revelation might say no, or prompt us to wait. Elder Neal A. Maxwell once noted that part of discipleship is learning that "God's thoughts are higher than our thoughts" (Maxwell, 1977, p. 16). That can be tough when we've prayed passionately for a certain blessing. Yet if we truly believe He sees the bigger picture, we can trust that a closed door might lead us to a better one down the hall.

Another aspect is accountability for what we do with our promptings. If the Lord nudges us to reconcile with someone or reach out to a struggling friend, we can't ignore it and then wonder why we aren't receiving more revelation. A pattern emerges: the more we act on the light we receive, the more light we're given. It's like building spiritual momentum. Conversely, ignoring promptings can dull our sensitivity to the Spirit, making it harder to hear the next time. This principle underscores why consistent obedience and repentance keep our spiritual ears attuned.

Sometimes, we expect revelation to solve all our problems immediately. But revelation isn't always about the end result; it's often about the journey. God might guide us step by step so we develop trust and endurance. Think of Lehi's family with the Liahona (1 Nephi 16, Book of Mormon): it provided direction day by day, not a fully mapped-out route. They had to exercise faith and diligence every morning to see where the pointer led. We, too, might receive just enough guidance for the next day or the next decision. That's how we learn to rely on Heavenly Father consistently.

What if you're in a place where you feel disconnected, as if the heavens are silent? It could be a sign to evaluate your spiritual habits. Are you praying consistently? Engaging with the scriptures? Attending church or the temple if possible? Are you allowing unrepented sin to block the Spirit? These are questions worth asking, not to shame yourself, but to identify any obstacles. Heavenly Father wants to speak to us more than we know, but He won't override our agency or persistent neglect of spiritual disciplines. Elder Henry B. Eyring once said that we "determine how close we will feel to God" by our decisions and efforts (Eyring, 2002, p. 109).

Let's not forget the role of spiritual confirmations that might have already occurred in our past. Sometimes we store up memories of times we knew God answered us, times the Spirit burned in our hearts. Keeping a journal of these moments can be immensely helpful for days when doubt creeps in. Elder Ronald A. Rasband calls them "spiritual markers" (Rasband, 2016, p. 82). When we reread them, we remind ourselves that God has spoken before, and He doesn't change. That can sustain our faith during quieter seasons.

In practical terms, learning to hear God's voice might look like this: You find a quiet moment each day (even if it's short). You open the scriptures and read, not just for information, but to find personal insight. You pray with an open heart, specifically asking, "Lord, what would You have me learn or do today?" Then you sit in silence for a bit. Maybe a thought comes to mind—"Text your neighbor and see how they're doing," or "Share a scripture with your younger sibling." Maybe you feel nothing, and that's okay—you keep going, trusting that over time, promptings will become clearer. Later, you might attend church or a Bible study group, and a speaker says exactly what you needed to hear. You recognize that as God's voice, speaking through someone else. You follow that counsel, and you notice peace in your life. That's how revelation can flow in normal, everyday experiences.

If you ever worry that you're not spiritual enough or you don't have the "gift" of revelation, please remember that Jesus said, "My sheep hear my voice" (John 10:27, KJV). He didn't say, "Only some of my sheep can hear me." We're all His sheep if we choose to follow Him. That means the ability to receive personal revelation is baked into our spiritual DNA. We just need to cultivate it. The Holy Ghost is a gift given to all who are baptized and confirmed, but even those who aren't formally members of a particular church can still feel the Spirit's influence. God is no respecter of persons; He can reach us wherever we are.

As you move forward in your quest to hear the Lord's voice, don't be afraid to make mistakes. You might think a prompting is from God, act on it, and realize later it was just your own wishful thinking. That's part of learning. Or you might sense a prompting but hesitate too long and miss the opportunity. That, too, is part of the learning curve. In either case, turn to Heavenly Father and humbly ask, "What can I learn from this?" Over time, you'll refine your ability to discern, much like tuning an instrument becomes easier with practice.

Ultimately, hearing His voice isn't about collecting cool spiritual experiences or bragging that you receive visions. It's about forging a relationship with Jesus Christ and Heavenly Father that is personal, daily, and transformative. The more we listen and act, the more our hearts align with Their will. And as that happens, we find ourselves living with greater peace, clarity, and purpose. We may not avoid every challenge—mortality guarantees bumps in the road—but we'll navigate them with the confidence that we're not walking alone. The same God who spoke to Moses, Elijah, Mary, and Joseph Smith can and will speak to you—in your own language, your own context, your own life.

So if you've been yearning to hear that still, small voice, here's your invitation: carve out time to be still, immerse yourself in God's word, pray with sincerity, act on the promptings you receive, and trust that even when answers seem slow, He's aware of every moment you wait. The heavens might feel silent at times, but they're never closed. There is a voice, gentle and steady, calling your name. As you learn to hear and heed it, you'll discover a Savior who's involved in the intimate details of your life, guiding you step by step toward His light and His love.

Chapter 12: Serving Others in Love

Imagine for a moment that you're watching a scene from a movie about a small town recovering from a disaster. People come together, roll up their sleeves, and lend helping hands. It's not an official holiday or an organized charity event—everyone is simply united by a desire to lift the burdens of others. There's a sense of warmth in the air, a shared energy that seems to say, "We're in this together." That same spirit can exist in our daily lives when we wholeheartedly embrace the principle of serving others. But service isn't just about the tasks we do; it's about the love behind the tasks. When we serve with love, we align ourselves with Jesus Christ in a powerful, life-changing way.

Sometimes we think of service as a separate category of spiritual duty—like, we have prayer, scripture study, attending church, and then there's service. But service is actually woven into every facet of the gospel. The Book of Mormon teaches that "when ye are in the service of your fellow beings ye are only in the service of your God" (Mosiah 2:17, Book of Mormon). That's a remarkable statement. It tells us that God views our kind acts toward others as if we were doing them directly for Him. If you think about it, that means every small, thoughtful gesture—every note of encouragement, every door held open, every genuine smile—counts in a big way to our Heavenly Father.

But let's also be honest: sometimes we're not in the mood to serve. Maybe we're exhausted, overwhelmed by our own problems, or simply uncertain about how to help. That's where we can remember that service isn't just about us; it's also about inviting the Savior's love into the lives of those around us. And ironically, when we do that, we often find our own burdens lifted. You might have experienced days when you felt down and decided to do something small for someone else—maybe deliver a treat or send an encouraging text—only to notice that your own spirits were unexpectedly buoyed. Elder Dieter F. Uchtdorf taught that "as we lose ourselves in the service of others, we discover our own lives and our own happiness" (Uchtdorf, 2010, p. 84). It's almost as if there's a spiritual equation at work: your sincere offering of love multiplies blessings for everyone involved.

We might also wonder whether our simple acts of kindness make a real difference in a world filled with large-scale problems—poverty, racism, addiction, abuse, you name it. The answer is yes, they matter more than we realize. Jesus Himself often ministered one-on-one. He stopped to heal individuals, talk to them, and invite them to follow Him. That's a blueprint for us. Maybe we can't eradicate hunger worldwide by ourselves, but we can help feed the neighbor who's struggling this week. Maybe we can't end loneliness for everyone, but we can be a friend to someone in our circle who feels isolated. No act of genuine care is ever wasted, especially if it's done in the spirit of Christlike love.

One of my favorite examples of service in the Bible is when the Savior washed His disciples' feet (John 13:4–17, King James Version). Think of the symbolism: here was the Son of God, the Creator of worlds, kneeling down to clean dirt off the feet of those He taught. It was an act of humility, a moment that flipped social hierarchies upside down. He was saying, in essence, that true leadership—and true discipleship—involves being willing to serve, even in tasks that seem menial. The surprising part is that Jesus didn't do this begrudgingly; He did it as a gesture of profound love. When we approach our everyday service with that same spirit, we catch a glimpse of the Savior's heart.

Maybe you're thinking, "That's nice in theory, but my life is chaotic. I'm barely keeping myself afloat." This is where the principle of "small and simple things" comes in (Alma 37:6, Book of Mormon). Service doesn't have to be grand or time-consuming to be meaningful. A sincere note of appreciation, a short phone call to check on someone, or a quiet prayer on behalf of a struggling friend can all be powerful forms of service. Elder M. Russell Ballard once suggested that sometimes the best service is "ordinary people doing simple things to help" (Ballard, 2012, p. 94). The important thing is the intent behind it—a desire to share the love of Christ in practical ways.

Let's not forget that serving others can also break down walls in our own hearts. Sometimes we carry grudges or judgments against others. We might think, "I can't stand that person" or "They've treated me poorly, so why should I help them?" But Jesus taught us to "bless them that curse you, do good to them that hate you" (Matthew 5:44, KJV). That's a tall order. Yet in the process of doing good—even toward those who may not deserve it by worldly standards—we experience a transformation within ourselves.

It's like an anti-venom for resentment. Each small act of service can chip away at our pride and open us up to the healing power of love.

Moreover, service can be a life raft for those in the midst of their own struggles. If you're battling depression, anxiety, or any heavy trial, focusing outward can offer moments of relief. It's not a magic cure—professional help might still be necessary—but it can create a healthier emotional environment. President Gordon B. Hinckley once counseled a young missionary who felt discouraged to "forget yourself and go to work," promising that he'd find greater joy in the process (Hinckley, 1984, p. 23). Many who have tried this approach—immersing themselves in acts of service—have reported that while their problems didn't vanish, they felt an increase in hope and resilience.

It's also important to realize that Heavenly Father can guide us toward who needs our help. If we pray each day, "Lord, please help me see someone who needs my help, and then help me be willing to give it," we might be surprised how often we're nudged in certain directions. That could mean sending a text to a friend we haven't heard from in a while, randomly delivering groceries to a neighbor, or even just giving a sincere compliment to someone who looks down. In these moments, we become instruments in the Lord's hands, carrying out His daily miracles. Elder Ronald A. Rasband taught that "the Lord works through our faith, and He works through our actions" (Rasband, 2016, p. 82). If we act on those subtle promptings, we can be part of something bigger than ourselves.

We should also talk about the role of boundaries in service. The Savior gave endlessly, but He also took time to pray alone, to rest, to commune with His Father. If you find yourself burning out or feeling resentful because you're overextending, it might be time to reevaluate. We're not called to run faster than we have strength (Mosiah 4:27, Book of Mormon).

Healthy service comes from a full heart, not a depleted one. If we sense we're on the brink of exhaustion, we might step back, refresh ourselves spiritually and emotionally, then return to giving. Service is about love, not martyrdom.

Serving doesn't just bless the receiver; it can spark a ripple effect. One act of kindness can inspire someone else to pay it forward. If you've ever read a story of someone paying for the car behind them in a drive-thru, you know how that often starts a chain reaction. The same thing happens spiritually when we do good. We set an example that can encourage others to step outside themselves. President Russell M. Nelson said, "We need each other. God designed that we would be interdependent" (Nelson, 2018, p. 46). Our interconnectedness means that positive actions spread more widely than we might guess.

That's especially true in families and close communities. Children observe how we talk about service—do we complain about visiting a sick neighbor, or do we model joy and gratitude in helping? Do we make time as a family to pray about who we can serve, or is that an afterthought? The choices we make in this regard can shape the next generation of disciples. By creating a culture of service at home, we instill habits of selflessness that last a lifetime.

Another element to remember is the connection between service and spiritual development. When we serve, we often feel the Holy Spirit more strongly. There's something about actively loving others that aligns our hearts with God's. It's like cleaning a window so the sunlight can pour in more fully. Elder Marvin J. Ashton once noted that service is "the rent we pay for living in this world of opportunity" (Ashton, 1992, p. 54). But more than that, it's the avenue through which we can experience a deeper communion with our Heavenly Father. We learn about His character by doing the things He would do if He were physically here.

If you're stuck on how to start, consider these practical ideas: – Write a note or send a text to someone going through a rough patch. – Donate time or resources to a local food bank or shelter. – Volunteer at church, whether that's helping with youth programs or cleaning the building. – Offer to babysit for a friend who needs a break. – Make a meal for a neighbor who's sick or overwhelmed.

None of these are earth-shattering, but each has the potential to bring real joy to another soul. And as you do them, remember to invite the Savior into your actions—offer your service as a form of worship. That changes it from an item on your to-do list to a sacred experience.

It's also okay to be creative. Not all service has to fit the mold of traditional charity. If you're artistic, you could create uplifting artwork to give away. If you're tech-savvy, you might help someone set up their computer or phone. If you enjoy yard work, you can help an elderly neighbor with their lawn. Heavenly Father gave us unique talents precisely so we can use them to bless others. And there's a special joy that comes from serving in a way that resonates with our own abilities and passions.

One caution: while social media can be a platform for good, we might want to check our motives. Are we posting about our service to glorify God, or to glorify ourselves? Jesus warned about doing "alms before men, to be seen of them" (Matthew 6:1, KJV). That doesn't mean we can never share good deeds online, but it does mean we should watch our hearts. Our main aim should be to lift others and honor God, not to rack up likes. The real payoff in service is the quiet satisfaction of knowing we followed the Savior's example—and the blessings of increased love in our own hearts.

Finally, let's consider the most fundamental reason for serving others: it's the essence of the two great commandments—love God and love our neighbors (Matthew 22:37–39, KJV). When we genuinely serve with love, we're fulfilling both. We're showing Heavenly Father that we appreciate His children, and we're blessing the very people He sent us here to learn and grow with. This life is about more than survival; it's about learning to become like Jesus Christ, and there's no better classroom for that than the field of service.

No matter your current struggles—addiction, loneliness, abuse, mental health issues—there's room for service in your life. And amazingly, as you serve, you might find your own burdens becoming more bearable. Heavenly Father hasn't forgotten you. He knows exactly what you're going through, and He delights in seeing His children support each other. If you feel unworthy or unqualified, remember that in God's eyes, a willing heart outweighs any perceived weaknesses. He can magnify your smallest efforts into something truly beautiful.

Service is more than an activity; it's a lifestyle of Christlike love. It's a daily decision to put compassion above convenience, to see people as beloved children of God rather than obstacles in our path. It's an invitation to step into the Savior's shoes for a moment and care for someone's wounded heart. That's the miracle of it—you and I get to share in the very work that Jesus Himself championed. And in doing so, we become more like Him—one small act of kindness at a time.

Chapter 13: The Atonement Is Personal

Let's talk about the Atonement of Jesus Christ in a deeply personal way. For many people, the word "Atonement" feels abstract—like a concept that applies broadly to the whole world but not necessarily to their individual struggles. But the truth is that Christ's Atonement is intensely personal. It's meant for you, for me, for every single person who has ever felt burdened by sin, heartbreak, illness, sorrow, or any of life's crushing weights. If you've ever wondered how the Savior's sacrifice applies directly to your individual pains and challenges, then this chapter is for you.

The Book of Mormon offers a beautiful insight in Alma 7:11–12, describing how Jesus would go forth, "suffering pains and afflictions and temptations of every kind," so He would know "how to succor his people." That term succor means to run to the aid of. It implies urgency and compassion. Imagine the Savior sprinting toward you, arms wide open, saying, "I understand every tear, every regret, every hidden fear, and

I'm here to help." That's not distant or impersonal—that's profoundly intimate.

When we talk about the Atonement, we often focus on the forgiveness of sins. And yes, that's a crucial part of it. Through Christ's sacrifice, we can repent, be cleansed, and ultimately return to live with Heavenly Father. But the Atonement also covers everything else that hurts us—the heartbreak from a relationship gone wrong, the grief of losing a loved one, the anxiety that keeps us up at night. The Savior's empathy for our pains is perfect, not just because He's all-knowing, but because He actually experienced the weight of mortal suffering in Gethsemane and on the cross (Luke 22:44; Matthew 27:46, KJV). That's why He's uniquely qualified to comfort us—He's been there in a way that defies our limited understanding of time and space.

Some might ask, "But how can one person feel all the pain in the world?" Honestly, it's beyond our mortal capacity to fully grasp. But we can trust the divine testimony of the scriptures and the power of God that transcends human limitations. One way to start embracing this is to think of it like a personal invitation: when you approach Jesus in prayer, you're not talking to someone who only vaguely knows your sorrow. You're talking to a Savior who has literally "borne our griefs, and carried our sorrows" (Isaiah 53:4, KJV). That means your shame, your regrets, your heartaches—He already felt the agony of those burdens and wants to lift them from you.

But we need to cooperate. The Atonement is a gift, freely offered, but we have to choose to accept it. That often begins with sincere prayer and repentance. We acknowledge our mistakes, ask for forgiveness, and commit to changing. And if our pain isn't tied to sin—like if it's a physical or emotional trial not of our making—we still reach out, inviting the Savior into our wounded hearts. Elder Jeffrey R. Holland taught that Christ "knows the way because He is the way" (Holland, 2006, p. 49). We can trust Him to guide us because He's already walked every path of suffering that exists.

One misconception is that we need to "have it all together" before we approach the Savior with our problems. That couldn't be further from the truth. Jesus ministered to the broken, the lost, the confused. He welcomed the sinners, the lepers, and the outcasts. He didn't wait for them to clean up their acts first; He reached out to them in their mess and then helped them become whole. The same principle applies to us: we don't have to present a polished version of ourselves at the altar of prayer. We can bring all our fears, doubts, and messy feelings. He understands. And from that raw honesty, true healing can begin.

Sometimes we wonder if our struggles are too small for the Savior's concern. We think, "Surely, He's got bigger things to handle than my everyday worries." But I love how President Thomas S. Monson put it: "There is no problem too small that it cannot be solved by the hand of the Lord, there is no problem so large that it cannot be solved by the hand of the Lord" (Monson, 2010, p. 77). The Atonement is infinite and eternal, covering both grand and seemingly trivial concerns. If it matters to you, it matters to Him. As we bring these issues to Him in faith, we'll often discover gentle reassurances or even specific solutions that we might not have considered.

Another important aspect of making the Atonement personal is realizing that Christ's sacrifice was not just a past event. Yes, it occurred roughly two thousand years ago, but its effects are ongoing and timeless. We sometimes see depictions of the crucifixion and resurrection as historical episodes, but we need to grasp that the power unleashed by those events is alive and relevant this very day. That's why we partake of the sacrament each week—to remember that His sacrifice continues to sustain us spiritually. President Russell M. Nelson taught that "the Atonement of Jesus Christ is the heart of the plan of salvation" (Nelson, 2017, p. 35). When something is at the heart, it means everything else circulates around it, draws life from it. That's how central the Atonement is to our daily walk.

It might help to think of the Atonement as a bridge spanning a great chasm. On one side is our mortal condition—our frailty, sins, and sorrows. On the other side is the presence of God—purity, peace, eternal joy. The Savior's love built that bridge so we could cross over. But crossing it is an active process. It's not automatic just because the bridge exists. We walk it step by step, day by day, repenting when we slip, relying on the Spirit for guidance, and clinging to faith in Christ's promise that He will see us safely across. Elder Tad R. Callister wrote that "the Atonement is not just paying off our debt; it is about changing our hearts" (Callister, 2011, p. 35). That means the journey transforms us, aligning us more closely with heavenly attributes.

For those wrestling with addiction or deep-rooted sin, the Atonement provides a way out that no self-help book alone can offer. Yes, we might need therapy, support groups, medication—these are all tools God can work through. But the spiritual dimension is irreplaceable. There's something about coming to Christ in humility, confessing our weakness, and pleading for divine strength that unlocks a level of healing we can't replicate on our own. Elder D. Todd Christofferson taught that "we are not merely trying to be better, we are seeking to become like Jesus Christ" (Christofferson, 2018, p. 62). That's a far deeper transformation than merely breaking a habit; it's a rebirth of the soul.

We should also note that the Atonement can heal wounds caused by others. If you've been abused or betrayed, you might carry deep scars. The Savior can address those scars, providing comfort and a sense of wholeness that transcends human understanding. You might still have memories and triggers—healing doesn't necessarily mean amnesia. But through Christ, you can experience a peace that reassures you that you're not defined by what happened to you. You're defined by your identity as a cherished child of God. That doesn't mean the path to healing is easy or quick. It often involves professional help, supportive friends, and a lot of patience. But the Lord's grace can undergird that journey, giving you the resilience to keep moving forward.

Some people fear that if they rely on Christ too much, they're being weak or shirking responsibility. The opposite is true. Relying on the Savior doesn't absolve us of effort; it invites us to partner with Him. We do our part—studying the scriptures, attending church, repenting daily, serving others—and He does what we can't: He sanctifies our efforts, multiplying their effect. Elder Neal A. Maxwell once said that "the submission of one's will is placing on God's altar the only uniquely personal thing one has to place there" (Maxwell, 1995, p. 35). Surrendering our will to the Savior is not a cop-out; it's an active choice to let His power refine us.

It's also worth remembering that the Atonement unites us in our weaknesses. We're all in need of the same redeeming grace, which means there's no room for looking down on others. When we grasp how reliant we are on Christ's mercy, we become more merciful to others. We realize that we don't stand on a higher pedestal; we're all kneeling at the feet of the same Savior. This fosters unity, compassion, and empathy within families, wards, and communities.

Let's address a practical concern: "What if I don't feel forgiven?" or "What if I can't feel God's love?" Emotional experiences vary, and sometimes we expect an immediate rush of peace. But sometimes it's more gradual, like a sunrise. You might not see the light instantly, but as you keep turning to Christ—praying, repenting, partaking of the sacrament, serving others—your heart begins to soften, and you sense a dawning of hope. Elder David A. Bednar taught that we shouldn't "expect instant miracles" but rather recognize that revelation often comes "line upon line" (Bednar, 2011, p. 50). The same is true for healing and peace from the Atonement.

If you're struggling with mental or emotional health challenges, the Atonement can also be a source of spiritual strength. It doesn't replace clinical treatment, but it can add a divine dimension of comfort and perspective. You can pour out your heart to the Savior, trusting He knows the agony of mental distress. In Gethsemane, He experienced anguish "sore even unto death" (Matthew 26:38, KJV). That means He can empathize with every form of pain, including those that aren't visible to the naked eye.

Sometimes, we might think the Atonement only kicks in after we've done all we can do, as if Christ is merely the "last resort." But the truth is, we need Him from the very first step. Alma 34:31–32 reminds us that "now is the time to repent," not after we've fixed ourselves (Book of Mormon). Trying to fix ourselves without divine help is like trying to drive a car with no gas in the tank. Sure, we can steer, but we won't get very far. The Lord asks us to invite Him into our efforts from the get-go, to lean on Him while we're still messy and uncertain.

On the practical side, making the Atonement personal might involve daily reflection. Maybe each night, you take a moment to ask, "Where did I see the Savior's influence in my life today?" or "How did I feel His grace helping me through a challenge?" By actively looking for His hand, you train your spiritual eyes to recognize it. You might even jot down these experiences in a journal. Over time, you'll accumulate a record of personal witness that Christ truly is at work in your life, assisting you in ways large and small.

Another powerful practice is to visualize yourself at the feet of the Savior, literally or metaphorically, placing your burdens in His hands. This isn't some new-age trick; it's a way to acknowledge that He is ready and willing to carry what we cannot. Matthew 11:28–30 extends that timeless invitation: "Come unto me, all ye that labour and are heavy laden, and I will give you rest" (KJV). That rest might not be a removal of our trials, but it can be a profound sense of peace within them. The difference is that when we're yoked with Christ, we no longer pull alone.

If you ever doubt whether the Atonement can cover "your brand" of sin or sorrow, remember that it was infinite in scope. "Infinite" means no expiration, no boundary. It encompassed every human failing, every heartbreak, every tear shed in loneliness. The price has already been paid; the question is whether we'll accept that gift. Elder Bruce C. Hafen wrote, "The atonement makes it possible for us to become the kind of people who can dwell in the presence of God" (Hafen, 1992, p. 19). That transformation is personal, intimate, and custom-fit to each soul.

At the end of the day, the Atonement is about a relationship—your relationship with the Savior. It's about letting Him into your daily life, not just at church on Sunday. It's about trusting Him with your joys and your sorrows, your triumphs and your failings. As you do, you'll find that He is far more compassionate and patient than you might have assumed. His heart is never closed, His arms never folded in rejection. Rather, He is the Good Shepherd who goes searching for lost sheep, rejoicing more over the one that returns than the ninety-nine already in the fold (Luke 15:4–7, KJV).

So if you've ever felt that your personal struggles are too complicated, or that your sins are too severe, or that your wounds are too deep, let the Atonement redefine what's possible. Through Christ, broken hearts can mend, addictions can be overcome, relationships can heal, and hope can flourish in the barren places of our souls. His grace doesn't just erase sin; it elevates us, turning us into better, holier versions of ourselves. And that transformation is available every day of our mortal journey.

I invite you—no matter where you stand right now, no matter how unworthy or discouraged you feel—to reach out in faith. Let the Savior prove to you that His Atonement is personal. Pour out your heart in prayer, study the scriptures that testify of His love, partake of the sacrament to renew your covenants, and watch how He begins to reshape your perspective. Over time, you'll see that He truly does know you by name, that He cares deeply about your daily struggles, and that He's already provided the means for you to find peace, healing, and eventually, eternal life with Him.

Chapter 14: Holding on to Hope Through Mental Health Struggles

Let's start by acknowledging something real and challenging: mental health struggles aren't a sign of weak faith. If you're dealing with anxiety, depression, or any other psychological or emotional challenge, it doesn't mean you're failing in your spiritual life. We live in a fallen world, and just like our bodies can get sick, so can our minds. The good news is that our Savior Jesus Christ and our Heavenly Father are big enough to handle all of it—the "perfect" versions of us and the very human, flawed, hurting versions of us. If you're in the midst of mental health battles, please know you're not alone, and you're certainly not outside the reach of divine love.

Many believers throughout history have experienced deep emotional turmoil. Think of Elijah, who felt so discouraged he prayed to die (1 Kings 19:4, King James Version). Or Hannah, who wept "in bitterness of soul" (1 Samuel 1:10, KJV) over her childlessness. Yet God did not dismiss them;

He ministered to them in profound ways. If you're wrestling with a mental health issue, you're in the company of many faithful people who have walked a similar road. This is not a club anyone really wants to join, but if you find yourself here, there's room for hope—and that hope is grounded in Jesus Christ's ability to empathize with and heal our deepest pains.

The Atonement, which we've discussed before, isn't just about forgiving sin; it's also about healing all forms of suffering (Alma 7:11–12, Book of Mormon). That means emotional and psychological suffering too. I know it might be hard to see God's hand when you're in the fog of anxiety or the darkness of depression. Sometimes it feels like your prayers ricochet off the ceiling. But even in your darkest moments, the Savior is closer than you realize. Elder Jeffrey R. Holland once said, "If for a while the harder you try, the harder it gets, take heart" because, in the end, "Heavenly Father rewards those who earnestly seek Him" (Holland, 2012, p. 31). That assurance reminds us that our effort to hold on—no matter how feeble it may seem—truly matters to God.

Now, let's talk about some practical steps. Faith and prayer are absolutely crucial, but we also believe in a God who works through earthly means. Just like we'd see a doctor for a broken arm, it's wise to seek professional help for mental health challenges. Therapists, counselors, and sometimes medication can be God's gifts to you—modern miracles that allow your mind and heart to find stability. Don't feel guilty if you need these tools. Elder M. Russell Ballard taught that we can "take advantage of professional counsel and medical assistance" while also seeking spiritual guidance (Ballard, 2010, p. 78). It's not either/or; it's both/and. The Savior can guide you to the right professionals, support groups, or resources that can make a real difference.

Sometimes, well-meaning friends might suggest that more scripture study or more prayer alone will "fix" you. But mental health is often more complex. Yes, staying close to God through prayer and scriptures can bring comfort, but it may not dissolve your depression or anxiety overnight. That doesn't mean you're spiritually lacking; it means you're dealing with a genuine mental or emotional condition that requires multiple forms of care. Think of it this way: if you're drowning, you need both the life preserver (professional help) and the outstretched arms of someone pulling you aboard (the Savior's love). They work together, and there's no shame in that.

The scriptures are filled with assurances that God is near the brokenhearted (Psalm 34:18, KJV). That includes hearts broken by sadness, trauma, or persistent worry. When you read these verses, try inserting your own name: "The Lord is nigh unto [your name] who is of a broken heart." Personalizing scripture like that can make it more tangible. We might also find comfort in the Savior's words: "Come unto me, all ye that labour and are heavy laden, and I will give you rest" (Matthew 11:28, KJV). Don't let shame convince you that mental health struggles disqualify you from that invitation. Jesus said all. That includes you—no matter how messy your thoughts or feelings might be.

Community support is another key element. Reach out to trusted friends, family members, or church leaders. You'd be surprised how many people have walked a similar path. They might not advertise it, but once you open up, you'll likely find you're not the only one facing these challenges. And if someone dismisses your struggles, don't let that deter you from seeking help elsewhere. Sometimes, people just don't know what to say or do. That doesn't invalidate your experience. Keep looking until you find supportive people who understand that mental health issues are real and deserve compassion, not judgment.

Service can also provide a sense of purpose and connection. Now, this isn't about ignoring your own needs; it's about recognizing that even when we feel broken, we can still bless others. Sometimes, a simple text message, a card, or a small act of kindness can give us a momentary break from focusing on our pain. It doesn't cure everything, but it can help us remember that we're still needed and that God can use us—even in our most vulnerable states—to be angels for someone else. The Lord has a remarkable way of sending comfort to us as we try to bring comfort to others.

Another aspect of coping with mental health struggles is learning to challenge unhelpful thought patterns. Prayerfully ask Heavenly Father to help you see yourself as He sees you—loved, capable, and precious. Elder Dieter F. Uchtdorf once said, "We are not ordinary. We are children of the Almighty God" (Uchtdorf, 2010, p. 86). Sometimes, depression or anxiety tells us lies like "You're worthless" or "There's no hope." Recognize these as lies. It's not always easy to challenge them, but with professional counseling and the guidance of the Holy Ghost, you can start to replace those false beliefs with truths about your divine nature and worth.

Self-care is another crucial element. Getting enough sleep, eating well, and finding time for restful activities might seem basic, but they set the stage for emotional stability. If your body is constantly running on empty, it's harder for your mind to find balance. President Boyd K. Packer taught that "the study of the doctrines of the gospel will improve behavior quicker than a study of behavior will improve behavior" (Packer, 1977, p. 25). While that's true for many aspects of life, it doesn't negate the fact that our physical well-being can affect our spiritual and emotional resilience. There's no shame in prioritizing rest or saying no to an overload of obligations.

Let's also acknowledge that answers to prayers might not come in the form we expect. We might pray for instant healing, but sometimes the Lord's answer is a series of small improvements over time—like a sunrise gradually breaking through the darkness. Elder David A. Bednar calls this the "line upon line" pattern of revelation (Bednar, 2011, p. 49). You might notice that, over weeks or months, you're feeling slightly better, or that certain coping strategies or medicines are working more effectively. That's the Lord's grace in action, even if it's not the lightning-bolt miracle we sometimes hope for.

If you feel distanced from God because of your mental health battles, try to remember that He's not giving you the silent treatment. Mental illnesses can numb our ability to feel spiritual emotions in the same way physical illnesses can limit our energy. Elder Ronald A. Rasband reassured us that "the Lord is aware of us, and He is mindful of our needs" (Rasband, 2016, p. 82). If you can't feel the Spirit the way you used to, don't conclude God has abandoned you. It could simply be that your mental state is muting those feelings. Keep praying, keep trying, and trust that the Lord sees your efforts even when you don't see or feel immediate results.

Sometimes, guilt or shame might creep in, making you think that if you just had more faith, you wouldn't be struggling. But consider this: even Jesus Christ felt deeply troubled in Gethsemane, to the point of sweating drops of blood (Luke 22:44, KJV). Was His faith lacking? Of course not. Suffering is part of the mortal experience, and mental health challenges are among the types of suffering some of us face. They don't necessarily indicate a lack of faith; they indicate that we're living in a fallen world where all kinds of trials exist.

Lastly, remember that your story is not over. The nature of depression or anxiety can make you think "This is all there is," but that's not true. There can be bright tomorrows, breakthroughs, and renewed hope. President Russell M. Nelson often speaks of the joy we can find in the gospel, even in difficult circumstances (Nelson, 2016, p. 80). It might not feel accessible right now, but don't rule out the possibility that your future holds more laughter, peace, and clarity than you can currently imagine. In the meantime, hold on to the truth that your Heavenly Father loves you, Christ's Atonement is big enough for every burden, and it's okay to seek help in all the ways God has provided.

If you or someone you love is experiencing severe symptoms—like suicidal thoughts—please reach out immediately to a mental health professional, crisis helpline, or trusted leader. This is not a lack of faith; it's a courageous step to preserve life and find help. Heavenly Father works through trained individuals who have the expertise to guide you through the darkest valleys. Let them help. No matter how dismal things appear, your life is infinitely precious, and Christ will walk this road with you step by step.

Chapter 15: Rediscovering Joy

We've talked about life's heavy burdens: abuse, addiction, loneliness, shame, mental health challenges, and more. It might be easy to think that this mortal journey is primarily about surviving trials. And yes, endurance is crucial. But there's also a shining principle woven throughout the gospel that can illuminate even the toughest times: joy. To some, that might sound like an empty platitude—"Just be happy!" But real joy in a gospel sense is far deeper than surface-level cheerfulness. It's a profound sense of peace and purpose that stems from our relationship with Heavenly Father and Jesus Christ.

Maybe you've heard the scripture that says, "Men are, that they might have joy" (2 Nephi 2:25, Book of Mormon). It's a hallmark verse we often quote in church lessons or personal study. But think about what that implies. Our Father in Heaven created us, placed us here with agency and a plan of salvation, all so we could ultimately experience joy. That suggests joy isn't just a bonus we hope to stumble upon; it's part of our eternal purpose. Yet, we might wonder, "How can I find joy when my life feels like a constant uphill battle?" The key is recognizing that joy doesn't necessarily mean the absence of trials; it means tapping into a divine reservoir of peace that can coexist with challenges.

The scriptures also teach that "the joy of the saints" comes from knowing God (Enos 1:3, Book of Mormon). When we talk about knowing God, we're referring to a personal relationship with Him, cultivated by prayer, scripture study, and sincere discipleship. Joy flourishes in that relationship, much like a plant thrives in sunlight. If we shield ourselves from the spiritual "sunlight" of daily connection with Jesus Christ, our joy can wither. But when we turn our hearts to Him—even in small, daily efforts—we invite the warmth of His love to permeate our lives.

This doesn't mean we ignore pain or slap a "grin and bear it" sticker on our grief. Rather, it's about learning to see God's hand even amid hardships. Think of Paul and Silas singing hymns in prison (Acts 16:25, KJV). They were literally in chains, yet they found a reason to rejoice in the Lord. We may not be in a physical prison, but mental or emotional prisons can feel just as confining. Still, when we shift our focus to gratitude for the blessings that do exist—a friend's kindness, a comforting scripture, a moment of calm—we begin to experience the subtle glow of divine joy. It may start small, but like a candle in a dark room, it can grow and push back the shadows.

Let's get practical for a moment. One way to cultivate joy is through intentional gratitude. President Russell M. Nelson suggested that expressing gratitude "turns our hearts to the Lord and helps us sense His love" (Nelson, 2020, p. 28). You might keep a small notebook or a note on your phone where you jot down a few things each day that you're thankful for. They don't have to be dramatic—maybe you enjoyed a sunrise, got an encouraging text, or noticed an unexpected solution to a problem. Over time, this practice can rewire your mindset to look for God's tender mercies. And as you notice those mercies, your sense of joy can blossom, even in the midst of struggles.

Another avenue to joy is creation. We're created in the image of a divine Creator, and often, when we tap into our creative side—whether that's art, music, cooking, writing, or something else—we discover a spark of delight that reminds us we're co-creators with God. Elder Dieter F. Uchtdorf famously said, "The more you trust and rely upon the Spirit, the greater your capacity to create" (Uchtdorf, 2010, p. 22). Creation can be a form of worship, a way to reflect the glory of God's creativity in our own lives. When we create something beautiful, we might feel a small echo of the joy God felt when He created the earth and declared it "good."

Service is another channel for joy. We've discussed the importance of helping others, but let's focus specifically on how serving can boost our own sense of happiness. There's something about stepping outside our own problems to lift someone else that reminds us life is bigger than our personal circle of worry. Elder David A. Bednar noted that "charity, the pure love of Christ, is manifested through ministering to others" (Bednar, 2014, p. 29). When that pure love flows through us, we often experience a divine satisfaction that transcends any momentary hardship. It's a bit like spiritual endorphins.

Of course, we can't forget the role of the Holy Spirit in bringing joy. Galatians 5:22 lists joy as one of the fruits of the Spirit (KJV). When we invite the Holy Ghost into our lives through righteous living, prayer, and sacrament worship, we're effectively opening our hearts to God's own peace and joy. This can manifest as a gentle warmth in our souls, or a sudden realization that, despite life's complications, we feel secure in God's love. That sense of security can be the bedrock of real joy. It doesn't require perfect circumstances; it only requires a willing heart and the presence of God's Spirit.

It's also helpful to remember that joy isn't always loud or exuberant. Sometimes it's quiet—like a steady flame in a windstorm that refuses to be extinguished. You might not be doing cartwheels of happiness, but you sense a calm confidence that God is in control, and that whatever happens, you are known and loved by Him. Elder Neal A. Maxwell described it as a "luminous" quality rather than a mere "flash of pleasure" (Maxwell, 1978, p. 89). This luminous joy can coexist with tears, with stress, and even with mourning. It might seem contradictory, but believers have testified that they can feel a spiritual joy mingled with sorrow, especially when they're grieving with hope (1 Thessalonians 4:13, KJV).

Another factor is recognizing that the Lord wants us to find joy in wholesome activities, not just strictly religious ones. Family gatherings, friendships, nature walks, hobbies—these can all be sanctified by a thankful heart. Elder D. Todd Christofferson noted that "God is a tender parent who would have you enjoy the good things of the earth" (Christofferson, 2015, p. 66). So if you feel a spark of joy playing with your kids or laughing over a silly movie with friends, that's not just frivolous; it can be part of God's gift of mortal happiness. The key is keeping our hearts aligned with goodness so that our joy remains pure and uplifting, rather than turning into indulgence or sin.

We should also address the reality that sometimes joy feels out of reach, especially if you're buried under severe trials or mental health struggles. That's okay. You don't have to fake cheerfulness. Instead, try to find small pockets of relief or comfort, trusting that the God of all creation sees your situation and has a plan to guide you through. Elder Ronald A.

Rasband taught that "the Lord works in mysterious ways but always for our ultimate good" (Rasband, 2017, p. 95). Sometimes, the knowledge that God is orchestrating something redemptive behind the scenes can give us a glimmer of hope—which can grow into a more sustained sense of joy over time.

If you're feeling guilty for not being "joyful enough," remember that we grow into joy. It's not a badge we earn by ignoring our problems; it's a process of learning to trust God's goodness even when life is messy. Elder Henry B. Eyring taught that "as we love God and trust Him, we open ourselves to a flowing of His Spirit that brings with it the happiness we desire" (Eyring, 1999, p. 105). Notice the verbs: love, trust, open. Those are actions we take, sometimes daily or even hourly, especially in stressful times.

One of the most vital lessons about joy is that it's deeply tied to Jesus Christ's victory over death and sin. The Resurrection stands as the ultimate symbol that sorrow, pain, and mortality's limitations don't have the final say. Elder Bruce R. McConkie once stated, "The most glorious, wondrous, and powerful event of all time is the resurrection of our Lord" (McConkie, 1972, p. 12). Because He rose from the dead, we have the promise of eternal life. That perspective can inject joy into even our darkest moments, reminding us that all earthly sorrows are temporary in the grand scheme of eternity. When we anchor ourselves in that eternal hope, our current setbacks lose some of their sting.

To invite more joy into your everyday life, consider building small spiritual habits. Maybe each morning you take 60 seconds to thank God for one specific blessing. Or each night, you reflect on a moment of light you experienced that day—even if it's as simple as seeing a blooming flower or receiving a kind message. These microhabits can gradually shift your outlook. Over time, you'll find that you're more attuned to the Lord's hand in your life, which naturally fosters a sense of joy and security. This doesn't negate real problems, but it helps you face them with a heart fortified by faith.

Another practical tip: surround yourself with uplifting influences. Music, art, friends, podcasts—whatever inputs you regularly have, check if they elevate your spirit or drag you down. President Thomas S. Monson once said, "Choose your friends with caution; plan your future with purpose" (Monson, 2008, p. 43). That advice extends to all media and relationships. We can't always avoid negativity, but we can be mindful and selective about what we allow to shape our thoughts. By seeking environments and content that reinforce gospel truths, we create fertile soil for joy to grow.

Lastly, remember that joy has a missionary dimension. When others see genuine joy in us—even amidst trials—they might wonder, "What's their secret?" That's an opportunity to bear testimony of Jesus Christ. We don't have to preach with a loudspeaker; sometimes a simple, honest statement—"My faith in Christ gets me through"—can resonate with someone who's searching. This doesn't mean we wear a mask of forced happiness; authenticity matters. But if we truly feel joy rooted in the gospel, sharing it can be an act of charity that points others toward the source of our hope.

In conclusion, joy is not a shiny sticker we slap on our problems. It's a fruit of our spiritual relationship with God, nurtured by gratitude, service, wholesome activities, and a profound trust in the redeeming power of Jesus Christ. Despite the pain and confusion that inevitably come in mortality, we can carry within us an unquenchable flame of hope. That flame is stoked each time we remember that "this life is but a moment" (Doctrine and

Covenants 121:7, 2013) and that our eternal future with our Heavenly Father and the Savior holds more light, love, and happiness than we can currently imagine.

Chapter 16: Loving Yourself as God Loves You

There's a remarkable scripture in the Bible that says we should love our neighbors "as thyself" (Matthew 22:39, King James Version). Usually, we focus on the "love thy neighbor" part, and that's important, but notice it also implies a healthy love for ourselves. If we're supposed to love our neighbors as we love ourselves, it means Jesus expects us to have at least some degree of self-love. Yet, for many of us—especially those of us struggling with feelings of unworthiness or shame—loving ourselves can feel like an uphill climb. We might believe Heavenly Father loves us, but do we really believe He sees us as worthy of our own love?

It's easy to mistake humility for self-neglect. We might think, "If I'm humble, I can't see any good in myself." But humility doesn't mean hating ourselves; it means understanding our true relationship with God—recognizing that He is our all-powerful Creator while also embracing that we are His precious children. Elder Jeffrey R. Holland once said that while we may not be perfect, we "have come unto Christ, and we are His" (Holland, 2012, p. 32). That means He claims us as part of His family, with all the affection and potential that implies.

Sometimes, negative experiences shape our self-image. Maybe someone in our life—family member, teacher, colleague—told us we'd never amount to much. Or perhaps we made a big mistake, and we've allowed that failure to define us ever since. But here's a gentle reminder: Heavenly Father defines us differently. He looks at each of us and sees a priceless soul with divine potential. Mistakes don't change that. In the Book of Mormon, we read that we're "free to choose liberty and eternal life" (2 Nephi 2:27), which implies we aren't stuck in our worst moments. We can keep growing, keep becoming, and keep reflecting the worth God has placed in us.

One of the hardest parts of loving ourselves is shutting off that inner critic. You know, that voice that says, "I'm not spiritual enough," "I'm not smart enough," or "I'm not good enough." Let me suggest an exercise: every time you catch yourself saying something harsh about yourself, stop and imagine how Jesus Christ would respond if you said it to Him. Would He nod and say, "You're right, you're no good"? Of course not. He would lovingly correct you and remind you that you have worth, that your future is bright, and that you're capable of more than you realize. Seeing ourselves through His eyes can be a powerful remedy for our self-criticism.

We also need to clear up a common myth: self-love is not selfish. Yes, selfishness is a problem, but it's totally different from healthy self-love. Selfishness is centered on pride and ignoring others' needs. Self-love, in a gospel sense, is recognizing that you're valuable because God says so—and therefore, you treat yourself with respect, kindness, and an openness to change and repentance. Think about it: if Heavenly Father truly wants us to inherit all that He has, as Romans 8:16–17 suggests, that means we're not meant to be spiritually bankrupt or self-hating. We're meant to be confident in His love and to reflect it in how we view ourselves.

Consider the Savior's command in Matthew 5:48 to "be ye therefore perfect." Sometimes we twist that into an impossible standard, berating ourselves every time we fall short. But in the Joseph Smith Translation and in modern scriptural contexts, the sense of "perfect" often means "complete" or "mature" in Christ (Nelson, 1995, p. 86). It's a process. Elder Neal A. Maxwell once said that God is more interested in our direction than our speed (Maxwell, 1979, p. 88). As long as we're honestly trying, He's pleased. Allowing ourselves to see that progress—rather than constantly fixating on our shortcomings—enables us to love the person God is helping us become.

There's also a correlation between loving ourselves and recognizing our divine heritage. The scriptures repeatedly call us children of God. Think of the love most parents have for their kids, then multiply that infinitely for how much God loves us. When we internalize that truth, we realize that demeaning ourselves is almost like insulting one of God's precious creations. If we truly value Heavenly Father, we'll value ourselves as His workmanship. That doesn't mean we ignore areas of improvement, but we approach growth with hope and optimism instead of self-loathing.

Practical steps can help. First, consider journaling. Each night, write down one or two things you did well. Maybe you reached out to a friend who was lonely, or you read a chapter in your scriptures when you didn't feel like it. Acknowledging these positive moments doesn't fuel pride; it fosters gratitude for the Lord's help and reminds us we're capable of good. Second, spend some time in prayer specifically asking Heavenly Father to help you feel His love. Elder David A. Bednar spoke of how revelation can come slowly, like a sunrise (Bednar, 2011, p. 49). Over time, you might notice your heart softening, a sense of divine acceptance filling the cracks in your self-esteem.

Another vital aspect is setting healthy boundaries in relationships. People who don't value themselves often let others mistreat them, thinking, "I deserve it." But if we see ourselves as God sees us, we realize we're allowed to stand up for ourselves. That might mean addressing disrespect or stepping away from harmful situations. It doesn't mean we stop loving others; it means we love ourselves enough to insist on respectful treatment. President Russell M. Nelson taught that "the highest compliment we can be given is to be called a covenant keeper" (Nelson, 2019, p. 44). Keeping our covenants includes respecting that we are sacred, and so we must ensure our environments and relationships honor that sacredness.

We might also think about the way we talk about ourselves in everyday speech. Little phrases like, "I'm so dumb," or "I always mess up," might seem harmless, but they can chip away at our self-perception. Try replacing them with softer language: "I made a mistake, but I'm learning," or "I'm still figuring this out." Over time, your brain starts believing the messages you feed it. It's not about ignoring reality; it's about framing reality in a way that aligns with God's perspective of growth and grace.

Now, what if you struggle with deep-rooted self-hate or shame because of trauma or repeated failures? Sometimes, professional help is part of the healing process. Therapy or counseling can work hand in hand with spiritual practices. It's not a failure of faith to seek help. Rather, it's an act of courage to say, "I'm hurting, and I need a safe space to process this." Elder Jeffrey R. Holland has repeatedly emphasized that God supports us in seeking professional assistance for mental or emotional challenges (Holland, 2013, p. 88). The combination of spiritual truth and therapeutic tools can dismantle negative beliefs and help rebuild a healthier self-concept.

We must acknowledge that self-love also involves repentance. Truly loving ourselves means wanting what's best for our eternal soul. If we're caught in sin, ignoring that doesn't reflect love; it reflects denial. The atoning power of Jesus Christ offers us a path to let go of destructive habits or guilt and move forward in forgiveness and hope. Through repentance, we align ourselves more fully with the Savior, and that alignment brings a sense of worth that no worldly accolade can duplicate.

Maybe you're wondering, "Won't loving myself make me complacent?" Not if it's grounded in the gospel. Real self-love motivates us to grow because we believe in our God-given potential. We realize the Lord wants us to be the best version of ourselves, so we strive for constant improvement. But our self-worth isn't tied to perfection right now; it's tied to our identity as children of God and our willingness to keep moving forward.

Living in a world that often defines worth by appearance, wealth, or accomplishments can be tricky. Social media can exacerbate this, as we compare our behind-the-scenes struggles to someone else's highlight reel. But remember, God's view of worth is entirely different. He's never impressed by superficial measures of success. He looks at our hearts, our desires, and our efforts. If we measure ourselves against His unconditional love, we'll find we already have immense value—even on days we accomplish nothing extraordinary by worldly standards.

Here's a final thought: the Savior's greatest commandments—to love God and love our neighbor—implicitly teach us about loving ourselves. As we see God for who He truly is—a loving Father who wants us to return to Him—we understand we're not random specks in the universe. We're beloved children. That perspective frees us to extend kindness not only to others but also to the person we see in the mirror. In short, "loving yourself as God loves you" is about discovering that being cherished by our Heavenly Father is the truest lens through which to view our own reflection. As we adopt that lens, we become kinder, more hopeful, and more resilient. That's the kind of self-love that honors God.

Chapter 17: Letting Your Light Shine

Think of a city on a hill at night, glowing so brightly that it can't be hidden (Matthew 5:14–16, KJV). That's the image Jesus used to describe those who follow Him. It's a vivid picture—light shining out in darkness, impossible to miss. But how often do we, as disciples, feel like our little flicker of faith is too small to matter? Or maybe we worry we'll come across as boastful if we let our light shine. The Savior's counsel, however, is clear: we're meant to be a light, not to glorify ourselves, but to illuminate the way for others to find hope in God.

You might wonder what qualifies as "light." In gospel terms, light can mean truth, goodness, love, encouragement—anything that points people to Heavenly Father and Jesus Christ. That could be your smile, your kindness to a stranger, your willingness to stand up for what's right, or your testimony shared in a quiet conversation. If you carry the gospel in your heart, you have a light. The question is, are you letting it shine?

One common hurdle is the fear of judgment. You might think, "Who am I to share my testimony? I'm no scripture scholar or perfect example." But sharing light doesn't require perfection. It requires sincerity. The Lord used flawed people throughout scripture to carry His message. Paul once persecuted Christians, Alma the Younger fought against the church, and yet both became bright lights in the world (Acts 9:1–22; Mosiah 27, Book of Mormon). Their credibility didn't come from perfect pasts; it came from their genuine relationship with Jesus Christ and their willingness to bear witness of His transforming power.

Another concern is the worry about coming off as self-righteous. Jesus addressed this too. He said to let our light shine so that others "may see your good works, and glorify your Father which is in heaven" (Matthew 5:16, KJV). Notice that the glory isn't meant for us; it's for God. When we do something kind or righteous, it's not about tooting our own horn. It's about reflecting the character of our Savior. If someone compliments you for your kindness, you can humbly acknowledge it while redirecting the praise to the Lord's influence in your life.

Letting your light shine can happen in everyday moments. Perhaps you notice a coworker who's struggling and quietly offer a supportive ear. Maybe you volunteer at a local shelter, or you let your social media posts focus on messages of hope rather than negativity. Elder Dieter F. Uchtdorf once said that the gospel should bring us joy, and if it does, it should naturally radiate from us (Uchtdorf, 2010, p. 84). That radiance isn't about being loud or pushy; it's about being genuine. When you love the Savior, it shows in how you treat people, how you handle stress, and how you remain grounded in faith during trials.

Sometimes, we think shining our light means we have to do something huge—like speak to massive crowds or start a worldwide charity. But Jesus ministered one by one. He stopped for individuals, listened to their stories, wept with them, celebrated their faith, and offered them truth. In our modern world, that same approach can still change lives. Maybe it's a text message you send to a lonely friend, or a ride you give to someone who has no transportation, or a family home evening lesson you prepare for your kids. Small acts, done with great love, reflect the light of Jesus Christ in ways we may never fully appreciate on this side of eternity.

Think about the people who have been a light in your life. Often, they weren't famous or flashy. Maybe it was a youth leader who listened without judgment, a neighbor who brought soup when you were sick, or a mission companion who taught you how to truly study the scriptures. Their acts might seem small in the cosmic scale of things, but they made a difference to you. That's the ripple effect of Christlike service. We never know how far the effects will go, but in God's economy, no loving act is wasted.

Letting your light shine also means not hiding behind a bushel of fear or shame. If you've felt intimidated to share your beliefs because you worry about backlash, remember that the gospel of Jesus Christ is called "good news" for a reason. It uplifts, enlightens, and promises redemption. Sharing it can be done respectfully and lovingly. You don't need to debate or be confrontational. You can simply say, "This is what I've experienced," or "This is how the Lord helps me get through tough times." Testimony, rooted in personal experience, often speaks louder than any argument.

We should also consider how letting our light shine intersects with our call to stand for truth. Sometimes, shining your light means defending gospel principles when society pushes against them. That can be uncomfortable. But remember, the light in you isn't a homemade lamp; it's fueled by the Spirit of the Lord. If you're prayerful and humble, you'll know when and how to speak up. Elder Jeffrey R. Holland once counseled us not to be "contentious," but also not to "compromise or dilute our convictions" (Holland, 2014, p. 45). That balance—bold but loving—resembles the Savior's own approach to teaching truth.

Another dimension is how your personal talents can amplify your light. Are you musically inclined? Then use that gift to inspire faith. Are you a good listener? Let that skill bless those who need a safe confidant. Are you creative in writing, design, or technology? Find ways to communicate uplifting messages. Elder Gary E. Stevenson taught that the Lord "needs you with your talents and strengths and your insights" (Stevenson, 2017, p. 52). Our individuality isn't a flaw; it's part of God's design. As we consecrate our unique attributes to Him, we become instruments for greater good.

You might also wonder: what happens if our light seems to dim? Life's trials can sometimes dampen our enthusiasm. Perhaps we go through a dark night of the soul—loss, illness, betrayal—and we feel our flame flicker. That's when we need to remember that Jesus Christ is the ultimate Light of the World (John 8:12, KJV). Our role is to reflect His light, like the moon reflecting the sun's rays. If we find ourselves in darkness, we can turn to Him for renewal. Regular prayer, scripture study, temple worship (when available), and partaking of the sacrament can refuel our spiritual lamp. President Russell M. Nelson likened daily spiritual habits to "daily drops of oil" that keep our lamps burning (Nelson, 2017, p. 36). Over time, those drops accumulate, and our capacity to shine grows.

Letting your light shine doesn't mean you'll never face criticism or opposition. Sometimes, people who prefer darkness resent those who carry light. But that's where courage comes in. Elder Dieter F. Uchtdorf has reminded us that "darkness cannot endure light" (Uchtdorf, 2017, p. 69). Eventually, truth and goodness prevail. In the meantime, hold fast to the

Savior, knowing that if He's asked you to be a city on a hill, He'll also provide the strength to keep shining even when the winds of adversity b low.

One practical idea is to pray each morning for opportunities to be a light. That might sound simple, but it aligns your heart with a mission mindset. You could say, "Heavenly Father, help me notice someone today who needs a bit of encouragement or truth, and guide me to act on it." Then go about your day with eyes open. You might find yourself prompted to compliment a coworker, share a scripture on social media, or offer a ride to someone. As you follow these nudges, you'll sense the Spirit's affirmation, and gradually, shining your light becomes a natural part of who you are.

Another tip is to avoid perfectionism in letting your light shine. We might think our efforts must be grand or flawless to count. But in God's plan, the small and simple things often yield great results (Alma 37:6, Book of Mormon). A heartfelt hug to someone grieving can be as important as a formal sermon. Let go of the pressure to stage elaborate acts of service or give polished monologues of testimony. Just be real, be kind, and be willing. The Holy Ghost can magnify your modest offerings in ways you can't predict.

If you struggle with shyness or anxiety, remember that shining your light doesn't always require public speaking or large crowds. You can let your light shine in quiet, personal ways—anonymously leaving a gift on a doorstep, writing a heartfelt note to a friend, or simply living in such a way that people sense the peace of Christ in you. St. Francis of Assisi is often quoted as saying, "Preach the gospel at all times; if necessary, use words." While we do believe in the power of bearing testimony verbally, there's wisdom in letting your daily life preach volumes about your devotion to the Savior.

Shining your light also means being open about your struggles and how Christ helps you through them. Sometimes, we think we can't share our faith unless we're problem-free. But vulnerability can be a beacon to others who feel alone in their trials. When we say, "I'm going through a rough patch, but I've found peace through prayer," it offers hope and relatability. Elder Holland once noted that we're all, in some sense, "unfinished symphonies" (Holland, 2012, p. 31), and that's okay. People often respond more to genuine transparency than to a polished facade.

In addition, letting your light shine can serve as a protective measure for your own faith. When you share what you believe, you reinforce those truths in your own mind and heart. Think about how bearing testimony in a fast and testimony meeting can strengthen you, even if you're a bit nervous. Elder Henry B. Eyring taught that "every time we bear testimony, we invite the Spirit to confirm the truth of what we say" (Eyring, 2008, p. 18). So there's a spiritual benefit for you as well as for the listener.

We also can't ignore that shining our light includes living the gospel principles in our personal conduct. If we profess one thing but live another, our light becomes confusing or even hypocritical. That doesn't mean we need to be perfect; it means we need to be sincerely striving to follow Christ's teachings. People will notice if we're trying. And even if they don't, our Heavenly Father sees our daily efforts, our small acts of obedience, and He honors them.

Lastly, remember that God called you to be a light in the exact time and place you're in. Elder Neil L. Andersen once said we were reserved for these latter days for a purpose (Andersen, 2009, p. 43). That means your unique talents, your social circle, your experiences—they all position you to influence specific people that someone else can't. Whether you're a student, a parent, a retiree, or anywhere in between, there are individuals who need the unique light you can offer. It might be a neighbor, a family member, a random stranger online—someone is waiting for your testimony, your kindness, your example.

So don't hide that light. Remember that even a small lamp can chase away the darkness in a room. Your flame might feel fragile at times, but if you stay connected to the Savior, it won't go out. The Holy Ghost can refill your spiritual oil daily, helping your light shine brighter than you ever thought possible. And in shining, you glorify not yourself, but the One who gave you that light in the first place. That's what it means to be a city on a hill—pointing every wandering traveler to the warmth and radiance of Christ's love.

Chapter 18: Holding On to Faith When Prayers Seem Unanswered

Picture yourself standing in front of a massive, ornate door. You can see light coming from the other side—warm and inviting—and you have every reason to believe something good awaits you beyond it. But as you knock, there's no obvious reply. You try again, perhaps louder, but everything remains frustratingly still. There's a part of you that wants to give up. Yet another part of you hopes that just maybe someone is on the other side, quietly listening. If you've ever felt that mix of uncertainty and longing, especially in your prayers, you're in the right place. This chapter is about those moments when we feel like heaven is silent, when we're not sure if we're heard, and how Jesus Christ and Heavenly Father fit into our experiences of seemingly unanswered prayers.

We talk a lot about how the scriptures are full of miracles—people being healed, seas parting, and prayers answered in dramatic ways. And yet, in our own lives, it can feel like we're playing a waiting game with God.

Some days, we might wonder if we missed the memo on how to get a direct reply. You're not alone in that wondering. Throughout holy writ, we also see faithful people who pleaded, waited, and sometimes questioned. We see Hannah praying fervently for a child (1 Samuel 1:9–20, King James Version). We watch prophets like Elijah, Moses, or Jeremiah each go through seasons where they had to wait on the Lord's timing. Even the Savior, in His great agony, asked if the bitter cup could pass from Him (Matthew 26:39, KJV). There's a pattern here: even those closest to God have had moments where the answer didn't come when or how they expected.

Let's break this down with real-life examples. Imagine a single mother who prays every night for a stable job so she can feed her children without worrying about rent each month. She's been sending out résumés left and right, trying to do everything "right," but no clear opportunity emerges. Another scenario: a college student prays to know which major to pursue. He prays morning and night, flips through scripture after scripture, and even fasts, hoping for a big "aha!" moment. Instead, he feels…nothing. In each case, the heart is sincere, the need is real, yet the heavens appear silent.

Why does this happen? Elder Neal A. Maxwell once famously said, "Faith in God includes faith in His timing" (Maxwell, 1991, p. 76). That implies there's more at play than just receiving immediate answers. Sometimes, the Lord is orchestrating a bigger plan we can't see yet. He might be shaping our character, teaching us resilience, or waiting for the right moment to reveal a blessing that will have maximum impact. Our perspective, limited to the present moment, can't always grasp the complexities of a divine timeline. Think about the story of Lazarus in the New Testament (John 11). Jesus delayed His arrival; Lazarus died. Mary and Martha must have felt that sting: "We asked for Your help, and You didn't come in time." Yet out of that wait sprang a miracle far greater than they initially imagined.

But let's be honest: knowing there might be a reason for the delay doesn't always soothe the ache. In the thick of it, we might question ourselves: "Am I doing something wrong? Did I not pray with enough faith? Does God not care about my situation?" That's when it helps to remember the Savior's empathy. He knows what it's like to feel a heaviness that doesn't lift immediately. In Gethsemane, He prayed multiple times, "If it be possible, let this cup pass" (Matthew 26:39–44, KJV), yet He still had to endure the Atonement's full depth. If Jesus Himself experienced waiting, even a kind of silence, we can trust that He comprehends every ounce of our frustration when heaven's response doesn't come promptly.

Another layer to consider is that sometimes we do receive an answer—it just doesn't match what we expected. Perhaps we prayed for a specific job, hoping that's the door God would open, only to sense a "no" or to face a closed door. That can feel like silence because we were so focused on getting a yes. Or maybe we prayed for relief from a particular trial, but instead of instant removal, we got strength to bear it or a sense of calm reassurance that we could endure a bit longer. We might write off that gentle reassurance as "no answer," when in fact, it was the Lord saying, "I'm with you, but this challenge stays for now."

We also need to address the issue of agency. Doctrine and Covenants 58:26–28 (The Church of Jesus Christ of Latter-day Saints, 2013) teaches us that we're not to be "compelled in all things." Often, God respects our ability to choose and figure things out. We might fervently ask, "Should I live in this city or that one?" and receive no definitive reply because the Lord is willing to let us decide. As long as we're not choosing sin or harming others, either path might be okay. In such instances, the silence we interpret could be God's nod that "Either option is acceptable; use your wisdom and move forward in faith." That can be disconcerting because we want a neon sign telling us exactly what to do. But part of our growth is learning to weigh options, counsel with the Lord, and then act.

Let's illustrate this with a personal anecdote: suppose you have two job offers. Both seem good. You pray, fast, and wait for an unmistakable spiritual prompting. Days pass; nothing. You might interpret that as God not answering. But maybe it's actually His way of saying, "You have prepared yourself. Go ahead and pick. I'll back you up if your heart is right." This concept underscores the idea that prayers are sometimes answered through our own reason and the gentle confirmations that come after we make a choice. We move forward with the best judgment we can, and then the Spirit either confirms or warns us if we're off track.

On the flip side, silence in prayer might also beckon us to change our approach. Elder Richard G. Scott said that to better hear the Spirit, sometimes we have to remove fear and replace it with faith (Scott, 2009, p. 45). If we're terrified God won't answer, we can become so wound up that we miss subtle promptings. Imagine being so anxious you can't hear a whisper. The Spirit's voice is often quiet, a still, small voice (1 Kings 19:12, KJV). If our mind is racing with worst-case scenarios, we might effectively drown out the Spirit's gentle guidance. A practical tip might be to calm ourselves with a brief moment of meditation or a deep breath before we pray, reaffirming that we trust God's ability to speak—even if we can't see how.

Another point is to recognize the difference between "no" and "not yet." If you pray about something that's not right for you, you might sense a strong "no." If you pray about something that's good, but not the right time, you might sense "not yet"—which can feel like silence. But over time, if you remain open and patient, clarity may emerge. Sometimes we need to let a situation unfold further. Think about the children of Israel wandering 40 years in the wilderness before entering the promised land. That's a long time to wait! Yet God had reasons—developing their faith, sifting out rebellion, and so on. For us, maybe it's not 40 literal years, but the principle stands: God's timeline can be longer than we'd like.

Now, let's talk about the feelings that come with unanswered prayer: doubt, discouragement, maybe even anger. Those feelings are normal. Faith doesn't mean never feeling frustration; it means turning to God even with that frustration. We can be honest in prayer: "Father, I feel alone. I don't understand why You're not answering me yet. Please help me trust You." Such raw honesty can actually strengthen our relationship with Heavenly Father. Think about biblical figures like Job, who openly questioned why he was suffering. The Lord responded, eventually revealing more of His majesty to Job, which deepened Job's humility and faith. Honest wrestling can lead to deeper connections if we stay engaged rather than walking away.

Let's also consider the possibility that God is answering, but in a different language than we expect. We might want a strong spiritual impression, but He might be sending help through a friend's timely advice or a random article we stumble upon. Maybe the answer to your prayer about finances comes through a workshop at your church about budgeting. Or perhaps your plea for emotional healing is answered by discovering a support group where you find camaraderie. If we limit God to one mode of communication—like a voice in our mind or a burning in our heart—we might overlook the variety of ways He can guide us.

Another factor is recognizing that sometimes, the Lord is quiet because He's testing how we'll act in the absence of overt direction. Elder Dieter

F. Uchtdorf once likened unanswered prayers to a teacher who remains silent during a test (Uchtdorf, 2014, p. 56). The teacher has already provided the lessons; now it's on the students to apply what they've learned. When answers don't come easily, we might have to rely on past instruction—scriptural teachings, previous spiritual experiences, or counsel we received earlier. This is a form of spiritual maturity: acting on what we already know while trusting that the Lord will correct our course if necessary.

If you're in a crisis—say, dealing with a severe illness, a broken relationship, or deep mental anguish—unanswered prayers can feel especially brutal. You might even start to doubt God's love or wonder if you're somehow unworthy. In those moments, remember that the Savior said, "In the world ye shall have tribulation" (John 16:33, KJV), but also promised that He has "overcome the world." This means the existence of trials, even crushing ones, does not signal God's abandonment. The Book of Mormon teaches that Christ descended below all things so that He might comprehensively lift us (Doctrine and Covenants 88:6, The Church of Jesus Christ of Latter-day Saints, 2013). Being lifted might still involve a timeline that feels excruciating, but it doesn't negate the final outcome of redemption and comfort.

Let's drill deeper into the mental health angle. Suppose you're suffering from severe anxiety or depression, and you pray daily for relief. Maybe you're longing for that immediate miracle—a sudden lifting of the darkness. Sometimes, God does grant miraculous healings. Other times, He points you toward a counselor, medication, or coping strategies. If we cling to the expectation of a purely spiritual resolution, we might dismiss the very solutions He's placing in front of us. Elder M. Russell Ballard emphasized the wisdom in combining professional assistance with spiritual practice (Ballard, 2010, p. 78). This synergy is often how God answers our pleas for emotional well-being.

It also helps to cultivate gratitude, even when you don't have all the answers. President Russell M. Nelson has talked about the power of sincere gratitude to unlock spiritual blessings (Nelson, 2020, p. 28). Writing down a few things you're thankful for each day can shift your perspective from what God hasn't given yet to what He's already provided. This doesn't magically solve your problems, but it creates an environment where the Spirit can more easily communicate, because you're focusing on God's kindness rather than your unmet desires.

Community support is another balm for times of unanswered prayer. When we feel like we're not hearing from heaven, we can lean on the testimonies of faithful friends or church leaders who've been in similar situations. You might find that someone else waited years for a particular blessing, only to see God's hand revealed in a surprising, beautiful way later on. Hearing their story can reignite your hope. The early Christians "continued stedfastly... in fellowship" (Acts 2:42, KJV). They understood that sticking together fortified their faith. We can follow their example by staying close to a spiritual community, whether it's a ward family, a small group, or just a couple of trusted believers who can encourage us in our faith journey.

Let's also not ignore the role of personal worthiness. Sometimes, unanswered prayer can be a wake-up call to examine our lives. Are we harboring unrepented sins, grudges, or consistent disobedience that might be blocking spiritual channels? God's love is unconditional, but the full measure of guidance from the Holy Ghost may depend on our willingness to live according to covenants and commandments (Mosiah 2:41, Book of Mormon). That doesn't mean every unanswered prayer is due to sin—far from it—but it's healthy to do a spiritual inventory. If you sense an area where you need repentance or improvement, addressing it can open new doors for revelation.

Yet, let's emphasize again: not all silence is about sin. The scriptures are filled with faithful folks who lived uprightly and still waited on the Lord. The waiting itself can be a crucible that refines us. Elder Henry B. Eyring once taught that there's a "law of increasing returns," where consistent obedience over time yields greater capacity to receive and recognize revelation (Eyring, 2007, p. 70). If you've only been praying for a short while, you might not have built that spiritual muscle to discern the Spirit's quieter nudges. Keep going. The more you pray, the more you learn the language of divine communication. Over months and years, you'll likely notice you can detect subtle answers that once seemed elusive.

In some cases, the greatest help is to simply remain faithful, even when it seems like no help is coming. That faithfulness can act as a testament that you trust God's character more than you trust your own timelines. Consider Abraham, who was promised countless descendants but waited until old age for Isaac to be born. If he'd given up, he would have missed the miracle. Or Joseph of Egypt, who spent years in prison, apparently forgotten, until he was raised up to a position that saved nations from famine. These scriptural examples aren't just stories; they're templates for how God often operates—through a seemingly impossible wait followed by a resolution that surpasses our expectations.

So, what do you do in the meantime—while you wait? Keep doing the small and simple things that invite the Spirit: pray daily, read the scriptures, attend church, partake of the sacrament, serve others, and maintain an open dialogue with God, even if you don't perceive an immediate response. Think of it like planting seeds. Each act of devotion plants a seed in the soil of your heart. You don't see immediate fruit the next day, but over time, those seeds germinate, sprout, and eventually produce a harvest of greater faith, insight, and yes—answers.

Be gentle with yourself along the way. Our Heavenly Father is not a stern taskmaster eager to catch you in a mistake. He's a loving parent who sees your genuine effort. Elder Jeffrey R. Holland said, "God is easy to please and hard to satisfy" (Holland, 2014, p. 45). That means even your imperfect attempts delight Him, but He also encourages you to keep growing. You might stumble in discouragement, skip a prayer or two, or lose your cool. Don't let that spiral into thinking you've ruined your chance at divine help. Just pick yourself up, apologize if needed, and continue forward. Each day is a fresh start in the eyes of your Redeemer.

Finally, never underestimate the quiet reassurance that can come from simply re-anchoring your faith in Jesus Christ's atoning power. The cross and the empty tomb stand as eternal witnesses that God can bring life from death, hope from despair. If He can conquer the grave, He can handle your unanswered questions. If He overcame sin and death, He can orchestrate solutions to your mortal struggles—though not always on the timetable you'd choose. This reality doesn't trivialize your pain; it frames it within the broader victory Christ has already secured. Understanding that can yield a type of peace that transcends immediate relief. It's the peace of knowing you're tethered to an all-powerful, all-loving God who will, in due course, make all things right (Revelation 21:4, KJV).

In the end, unanswered prayers aren't about God ignoring you. Often, they're about Him guiding you to deeper trust, broader perspective, and a more intimate understanding of His ways. That doesn't mean you're "failing" spiritually; it might mean you're exactly where you need to be for a future blessing that's bigger than your current request. So, keep knocking on that door. Keep praying, studying, serving, repenting, and believing. Even if your knuckles are sore from knocking, even if the silence continues longer than you'd like, trust that your Savior stands on the other side, aware of every knock and every tear, ready to open the door at the perfect moment. And when He does, you might just find that the blessing behind it far exceeds what you initially prayed for.

Chapter 19: Looking to the Savior in Every Season

Life is full of seasons, both literal and metaphorical. We have phases of youth, adulthood, middle age, and our senior years. We experience seasons of rapid change—like missions, marriage, or new jobs—and seasons of relative stability. Each season brings unique challenges and blessings. But one thing is constant through all of them: Jesus Christ remains the same, "yesterday, and to day, and for ever" (Hebrews 13:8, KJV). In an ever-shifting world, that's a tremendous source of comfort.

In your teenage years, you might feel an urgency to define who you are. Peer pressure, academic demands, and questions about the future swirl around you. It can be chaotic. Yet, the Savior beckons, "Come unto me" (Matthew 11:28, KJV), offering rest from the pressures of worldly expectations. If you learn early to rely on Him, you establish habits—prayer, scripture study, church attendance—that set a solid foundation for the decades to come. Elder David A. Bednar taught that young people who anchor themselves in gospel truths can "stand steadfast and immovable" despite the storms of adolescence (Bednar, 2009, p. 25).

When we move into adulthood, responsibilities multiply. Perhaps we're juggling careers, raising children, or facing financial stress. In this season, it's easy to lose sight of spiritual priorities because life feels so busy. But Jesus isn't just for quiet Sunday mornings; He's for every day, in the hustle and bustle of errands, deadlines, and soccer practices. Elder D. Todd Christofferson counseled that "a consecrated life respects the diversity of ways in which disciples may serve" (Christofferson, 2010, p. 63). That means we don't have to compartmentalize our faith; we can integrate gospel principles into how we work, how we parent, and how we treat neighbors. Inviting the Lord into the hectic routine can transform mundane tasks into acts of devotion.

As we move into midlife, we might find ourselves caring for aging parents, supporting grown children, or navigating career changes. It can be a season of recalibration, sometimes marked by questions like, "Have I accomplished enough?" or "What is my purpose now?" The answer, again, can be found in our relationship with Heavenly Father. President Russell M. Nelson taught that "there is no age barrier when it comes to serving the Lord" (Nelson, 2018, p. 46). If we seek His will, we might discover new ways to minister—perhaps mentoring younger generations, volunteering in community service, or becoming a more intentional grandparent. The Lord has work for us in every chapter of our story.

Then there are the later years, when bodies slow down and the horizon of mortality comes into view. This can be a time of rich spiritual reflection, as we look back on how the Savior guided us. However, it can also be a season of loss—losing friends, dealing with health issues, or feeling less "useful." Yet, even here, Christ stands by us. The prophet Isaiah promises that God will carry us "even to your old age" (Isaiah 46:4, KJV). Elder Robert D. Hales once explained that older adults can still offer vital contributions—through wisdom, testimony, and quiet acts of love that ripple far beyond what they see (Hales, 1998, p. 36).

Of course, the seasons of life aren't strictly tied to age. You could be in a "winter" season during your twenties if you're facing depression or job loss. Or you might experience a bright "summer" season in your sixties if life is stable and blessings abound. The key is recognizing that Jesus Christ stands ready to walk with us in every stage—celebrating our joys and comforting us in our sorrows. Just as the earth cycles through different climates, our lives ebb and flow with transitions. But the One who created this earth is intimately familiar with all cycles, all phases, all emotional climates. He can be our constant, our center.

One pitfall is thinking, "I'll be happy once I get past this season." If we're single, we might think marriage is the golden ticket. If we're overwhelmed parents, we might long for an empty nest. If we're older, we might yearn to recapture youth. But tying our happiness to the next milestone can cause us to miss the blessings of the here and now. Jesus taught, "I am come that they might have life, and that they might have it more abundantly" (John 10:10, KJV). That abundance is available now, not just after some future change. Elder Dieter F. Uchtdorf often emphasizes living in the present with gratitude (Uchtdorf, 2008, p. 18). We can find purpose in each season by asking, "Lord, what would you have me learn and do in this very moment?"

We also face spiritual seasons—times of closeness to God and times of distance. Sometimes we're on a "spiritual high," eager to serve, read scriptures, and share our testimony. Other times, we might feel dry or disconnected. If you're in a spiritual winter, don't panic. Seasons change. Keep doing the basics—praying, studying, attending church—and trust that spring will come again. Elder Ronald A. Rasband taught that "disciples of Jesus Christ remain faithful, even in times of uncertainty or adversity" (Rasband, 2017, p. 95). God hasn't abandoned you in your spiritual slump. Sometimes He allows such periods to deepen our dependence on Him and refine our faith.

In any season—literal or spiritual—we can find ways to serve. Maybe you're a busy parent, but you can volunteer a few hours at a soup kitchen or lead a youth activity at church. If you're retired with time on your hands, you might mentor someone in your ward or community. If your mobility is limited, you can pray for others, make phone calls, or send encouraging notes. Service transcends age or circumstance. In fact, it often brings a renewed sense of purpose that brightens whatever season we're in.

Also, never underestimate the power of reflection. Looking back can reveal God's hand in past seasons, which bolsters our faith for the season we're in now. Elder Dieter F. Uchtdorf has spoken about how personal history can teach us gratitude and insight (Uchtdorf, 2010, p. 86). You might see that God led you to certain people or experiences at just the right time. Or you might realize that a painful detour was actually a blessing in disguise. These realizations can help you embrace your current season with more trust in God's plan.

If you're someone who doesn't like change—who'd prefer a permanent status quo—take courage in knowing that Jesus is the anchor in life's transitions. Nothing catches Him by surprise. He guided the children of Israel through the wilderness for forty years, adapting their circumstances along the way. He can guide you through new jobs, relocations, marriages, divorces, illnesses—whatever arises. Elder M. Russell Ballard taught that "change is an essential part of God's plan" (Ballard, 2005, p. 74). That might be unsettling, but it's also comforting to realize that each stage of life is an opportunity for fresh growth and new demonstrations of God's faithfulness.

If we approach each season with humility and a willingness to learn, we might find that the Lord uses these varying phases to mold us into more compassionate, empathetic disciples. A teenage heartbreak could later become a reference point for comforting a niece or nephew going through the same thing. A midlife crisis could turn into a profound spiritual recalibration. An older adult's loneliness could lead to deeper conversations with God than ever before. The point is, no season is wasted if we invite Christ to walk it with us.

Above all, remember that our ultimate season is eternal life with Heavenly Father. Mortality is just one chapter in an infinite story. This perspective can calm our anxieties about aging, regrets, or missed opportunities. Elder Joseph B. Wirthlin famously said, "Come what may, and love it" (Wirthlin, 2008, p. 27). That's not a call to enjoy every trial, but to trust that each season is part of our journey toward a glorious eternity. When we see things through an eternal lens, we're more patient with ourselves and more open to the lessons each season offers.

So whatever your current season—young or old, thriving or struggling—know that Jesus Christ meets you where you are. He understands your joys, sorrows, and uncertainties. Lean on Him as you navigate the changes, and you'll discover that each new phase has the potential to deepen your testimony and draw you closer to God's ultimate plan for you.

Chapter 20: Embracing Your Divine Heritage

Imagine sitting on a quiet beach, watching the tide roll in. The water ebbs and flows, never staying in one place, but always guided by something bigger—gravity, the moon, the vastness of the ocean itself. Now consider your own life's journey: there are ups and downs, ebbs and flows, times you feel anchored, and times you feel adrift. Yet no matter what you experience, a profound truth remains: you are, first and foremost, a child of God. Embracing that divine heritage can feel like discovering a hidden treasure that's been yours all along. For some, it's a new revelation; for others, it's a gentle reminder. Either way, it has the power to shape how you see yourself, others, and even your darkest trials.

It's one thing to casually say, "I am a child of God," and another to let that truth seep into your heart so deeply that it changes your everyday choices. Think about what it means for your self-worth. If you're a child of God, you have infinite, built-in value. No amount of external validation—or lack thereof—can alter that. If someone disapproves of you, or if you fail at some endeavor, it doesn't redefine who you are. You remain a cherished soul in the eyes of your Heavenly Father. Elder Dieter F. Uchtdorf taught that God's love "is simply always there" (Uchtdorf, 2009, p. 75). Always. That means on your worst hair day, your worst sin day, your worst everything day, your divine DNA remains intact.

That perspective can realign how you view your worthiness to pray, to serve, or even to hope for blessings. Sometimes we think, "I'm too flawed for God to listen," but if you're His child, He's already invested in you—like a perfect parent who never tires of hearing your voice. Prayer stops feeling like a formal request form and starts feeling like a conversation with someone who truly gets you. Of course, you still approach Him with reverence, but that reverence is mingled with a sense of belonging. You are not a stranger knocking on the door of a distant King; you're a child walking into your Father's presence.

Embracing your divine heritage also reshapes how you see other people. If you grasp that you're God's child, then you realize every other person you meet is, too. The grumpy neighbor, the relative who hurt you, the coworker who drives you crazy—they all share that same spiritual parentage. That doesn't mean you ignore boundaries or allow mistreatment, but it does mean your ability to forgive and show compassion can widen. Elder Jeffrey R. Holland reminded us that no one is beyond the reach of the Atonement (Holland, 2012, p. 31). Recognizing divine heritage in others softens our hearts, helping us see them through a lens of empathy.

In the Book of Mormon, we find a verse that says, "The Spirit itself beareth witness... that we are the children of God" (Romans 8:16, King James Version, also reflected in 2 Nephi 9–10 commentary). That's a bold statement—God Himself wants to confirm that identity within us. One way He does that is through the Holy Ghost. Have you ever felt a warm sense of reassurance that you're loved, despite your failings? That might be the Spirit testifying of your divine lineage. On the flip side, the adversary tries to convince you that you're just another flawed human, unimportant and destined to fail. But the devil's argument crumbles when weighed against the truth that you come from an eternal pedigree.

This truth becomes even more powerful when we think about potential—who we can become. If we're offspring of a perfect, exalted Being, what does that say about our future prospects? President Russell M. Nelson taught that our Heavenly Father "wants you to live with Him again" (Nelson, 2018, p. 42). He's not merely tolerating our presence in heaven; He's inviting us to inherit all that He has (Romans 8:17, KJV). That inheritance includes the capacity to grow in wisdom, love, creativity, and holiness. Yes, it's a long journey, but it's a trajectory defined by limitless upward mobility. Once you grasp that, the daily grind of life takes on a new sense of hope. Obstacles become stepping-stones rather than insurmountable walls.

Still, it's easy to forget our divine heritage in the stress of living. We get bogged down by work deadlines, family dramas, health concerns, and financial woes. We might think, "If I'm really a child of God, why is life so hard?" That's a fair question. But consider that even in earthly terms, parents who love their children allow them to face challenges because overcoming them builds resilience. Our Heavenly Father's plan for us includes growth, and growth often sprouts in the soil of adversity. Elder Orson F. Whitney once wrote that no trial is wasted if it brings us closer to God (Whitney, 1921, p. 57). Embracing your divine heritage doesn't mean an easy life; it means a meaningful one, where each hurdle can refine you into someone more Christlike.

Another dimension of this concept is how it counteracts shame. We discussed shame in a previous chapter, but it's worth reiterating that if you are truly a child of God, shame has less room to fester. Shame says, "You are defective." Divine heritage says, "You are chosen, loved, and capable of redemption." Guilt might remind you that you made mistakes, but it never erases your identity as God's offspring. Your spiritual DNA isn't canceled out by sin; it's something the Atonement can restore to full brightness as you repent. Elder Dieter F. Uchtdorf once pointed out that God never gives up on us, and we shouldn't give up on ourselves (Uchtdorf, 2010, p. 23).

To internalize your divine heritage, it can help to deliberately nurture your relationship with Heavenly Father. Prayer is one avenue, of course. Instead of reciting a checklist of blessings and requests, consider having a heart-to-heart with God about your insecurities, your questions, your hopes. Sometimes, you might just sit in silence, letting the Spirit permeate your thoughts. Scripture study is another way. Look for verses that highlight God's love for His children—like John 3:16 or 1 John 3:1. Let those words sink in until they feel personal. Meditation or quiet reflection can also be a conduit. Even service, especially when done with pure intent, can open your heart to the divine worth of both yourself and those you serve.

Think about times when you felt closest to God. Maybe it was a church camp, a spiritual retreat, or a quiet evening at home. What was different about that moment? Often, it's that you were less distracted, more open, and more focused on heavenly things. Those moments are like signposts reminding you of your true nature. They're hints that we're all spiritual beings having a mortal experience, rather than mortals occasionally having spiritual moments. Elder Neal A. Maxwell taught that the more we see our eternal identity, the more we can navigate life's trials with faith (Maxwell, 1974, p. 12).

Embracing your divine heritage also invites you to ask, "Am I living in a way that honors my birthright?" When we realize we're children of a perfect Father, we might feel a pull to align our actions with that truth—like a prince or princess who behaves responsibly because they represent the royal family. This isn't about guilt-tripping ourselves into forced obedience; it's about living with integrity because we see ourselves as part of God's family. That perspective can shift how we treat our bodies, how we engage in relationships, and how we handle moral dilemmas. Instead of grudgingly checking off commandments, we begin to see obedience as a reflection of who we really are.

At times, you might feel overwhelmed by how short you fall compared to God's perfection. That's where the Savior's grace enters. Jesus Christ didn't perform the Atonement so you could prove your worth; He did it because you're already of worth to Him. Embracing your divine heritage isn't a performance test—it's a realization that your identity is secure in God's eyes, and the Savior's sacrifice bridges the gap between your current state and your eternal destiny. Elder Jeffrey R. Holland said, "We get credit for trying, even if we don't always succeed" (Holland, 2002, p. 96). In a world that demands perfection, God looks at your heart's desire to follow Him.

Consider this practical approach: each day, look in the mirror—literally—and say, "I am a child of God, and He loves me." It might feel odd at first, but repeating that phrase can reinforce the truth you're striving to internalize. Over time, that affirmation can transform how you think. Another approach is to write a letter to Heavenly Father, detailing your fears and dreams, then read it out loud, imagining His gentle response: "My child, I'm proud of your efforts, and I'm here to guide you."

These small activities can solidify a spiritual perspective that the world's noise often drowns out.

Embracing your divine heritage is also about receiving love from others who carry the same divine spark. Fellowship with believers, whether in church or other settings, can strengthen your sense of belonging to God's family. When someone testifies of the gospel in sacrament meeting, it can resonate with the part of you that knows you're connected to Heavenly Father. Serving side by side with others who share this belief can remind you that you're not just an isolated soul trying to be "good enough." You're part of a grand community of God's children, each with a unique role to play.

If you find yourself questioning whether you really have a divine heritage, maybe because life has been harsh or because your past is full of regret, consider the powerful examples in scripture. Alma the Younger was "the very vilest of sinners" (Mosiah 28:4, Book of Mormon) before his dramatic conversion. The Apostle Paul went from persecuting Christians to being one of the most influential early church leaders. Their histories didn't erase their divine identity; God's love and the Savior's Atonement reclaimed it. That same redemption is available for you. No matter how tangled your journey has been, your heritage remains a beacon guiding you toward a brighter horizon.

Ultimately, recognizing you are God's child is a game-changer for how you handle adversity. Problems don't magically vanish, but you face them with the calm assurance that you're not just some random mortal battling impossible odds. You're a divine spirit temporarily clothed in mortality, and your Heavenly Father is cheering you on from beyond the veil. That knowledge can kindle hope in the darkest hours, turning despair into a quiet confidence that, come what may, you still belong to the greatest family in the universe.

May you hold fast to that truth. May it light your path when you feel lost, uplift you when you feel unworthy, and inspire you to love others who share this sacred origin. This is your birthright: to know that you matter profoundly to a loving Father and that your journey is leading you back to His presence. Embrace it, and watch how it transforms your perspective, your relationships, and ultimately, your soul.

Conclusion & Final Invitation

We've journeyed through countless topics in this book, from overcoming abuse, addiction, and loneliness to grappling with shame, mental health issues, and the trials that test our faith. Through every theme, one core truth has remained constant: you are a cherished child of Heavenly Father, and Jesus Christ's love for you is beyond measure. Life throws every kind of curveball—sometimes it feels like you're balancing a dozen of them at once—but the Savior's arms are always outstretched, ready to catch you when you stumble or carry you when you're too weary to walk.

If there's one takeaway I hope you tuck into your heart, it's that you don't have to face your challenges alone. Yes, we live in a world that demands grit and perseverance, but true grit is found in leaning on the Lord. The scriptures teach that in Jesus Christ, we find "rest" (Matthew 11:28, KJV), not because life stops being hard, but because He shares our burdens. Whether you're wrestling with trauma, fighting an addiction, drowning in loneliness, or simply feeling disconnected from God, the Savior is there, whispering, "Come unto me." Those words aren't just for the "righteous" or the "worthy"; they're for every soul who recognizes their need for Him—which, let's be honest, is all of us.

I know this book won't stop the pain or erase the loneliness. It won't solve your problems. That's the point of life—it's a journey. And journeys take time. My goal wasn't to offer easy answers but to remind you of a profound truth: you are loved by He who created everything. The One who set the stars in the heavens and calls them by name also knows your name. You are thought about constantly by He who can count the grains of sand on every beach, who sees your struggles, and who treasures your effort, no matter how small it feels.

If nothing else, I hope this book serves as a gentle nudge to help you see that love, even in the moments when it feels far away. It's there, always. And as you lean on the Lord, trusting in His timing and infinite care, you'll discover that the journey—difficult though it may be—is where His grace and your growth meet in a way that changes everything.

Throughout these chapters, we've also highlighted the importance of practical help. Sometimes, the most faithful thing you can do is call a counselor, reach out to a friend, or even dial emergency services if you're in crisis. Prayer and priesthood blessings are vital, but they can coexist with therapy, medication, support groups, or a trusted mentor's advice. The Good Samaritan didn't just say a prayer over the wounded man; he bandaged him, took him to an inn, and paid for his care (Luke 10:34–35, KJV). Heavenly Father often works through the hands of those around us, so don't hesitate to let them help.

As you reflect on your own struggles, remember that your worth is fixed in God's eyes. It doesn't diminish with each mistake or waver with each trial. You are the "offspring of God" (Acts 17:29, KJV). From the moment He formed your spirit, He saw potential in you that surpasses your wildest dreams. If you've never felt that kind of love—maybe because of past abuse or negative self-talk—know that it's real and constant, waiting for you to uncover it. The more we internalize our divine identity, the less power the adversary has to keep us stuck in discouragement or sin.

We've discussed shame and forgiveness, too. Let me reiterate: no sin is beyond the scope of Christ's Atonement, and no wound is too deep for His healing. Repentance isn't a punishment; it's a gift that lets us shed our burdens and walk freely again. If you carry shame for something that happened years ago or even yesterday, take it to the Lord. He specializes in cleansing hearts. The process might not be overnight—true healing rarely is—but step by step, He will help you rebuild your life on a foundation of mercy and grace. Elder Jeffrey R. Holland once reminded us that Christ "is not waiting for us to be perfect" before extending His love (Holland, 2012, p. 31). That's the best news we could ever receive.

We've also explored the idea of serving others, shining our light, and recognizing the beauty in different seasons of life. These aren't disconnected topics; they interweave into a life spent following Jesus Christ. As you strive to lighten someone else's load, your own burdens become more bearable. As you let your gospel light shine, you bless others and reinforce your own faith. As you embrace each season with the Savior's guidance, you transform challenges into stepping-stones of spiritual growth. We're not meant to be passive spectators in mortality; we're invited to be active participants in God's work—His work of healing, teaching, and loving.

Ultimately, this entire journey circles back to a single truth: You Are His Child. That simple phrase anchors everything. When storms rage, when doubts creep in, when relationships falter, or when your own thoughts turn dark—remember that your identity is secure in the Lord's eyes. You can't outrun His love, you can't disqualify yourself from His grace, and you can't sink below the infinite reach of His atoning sacrifice (Doctrine and Covenants 88:6, The Church of Jesus Christ of Latter-day Saints, 2013). Even in the throes of your worst day, He sees the best in you.

As we part ways in this book, my prayer is that you'll carry a renewed sense of hope. Not a superficial optimism that everything will always go right, but a deeply rooted faith that, come what may, you're not alone. You belong to a Heavenly Father who orchestrated a plan that includes both trials and triumphs. You have a Savior who walked a path of suffering so you wouldn't have to walk yours alone. You're supported by the Holy Ghost, who whispers truth in the quiet corners of your heart. And you're surrounded by fellow travelers—some may be in your church or family, others you'll meet unexpectedly—who can share your burdens if you let them.

If you ever find yourself forgetting these truths—because, let's face it, life has a way of clouding our vision—return to the basics. Pray, even if all you can do is utter a single sentence. Open the scriptures, even if you read just one verse. Serve someone else, even if it's the smallest act of kindness. Each of these simple actions invites the Spirit to confirm what you've known all along: that you are loved, you are wanted, you are remembered and you have a purpose.

Above all, never lose sight of the reality that Jesus Christ's love is not a generic form letter. It's personal and directed at you. He knows your name, your story, and your silent heartaches. He offers the same invitation He's offered throughout generations: "Come unto me." I testify that as you accept that invitation—day by day, choice by choice—you will discover a wellspring of courage and peace you never knew you had. Your journey might not become easy, but it becomes hopeful, purposeful, and deeply fulfilling.

Thank you for letting me walk alongside you through these pages. Thank you for being willing to consider the possibility that you are, indeed, His child—precious, redeemed, and limitless in potential. My closing thought is a simple one: Embrace the truth of who you are, whose you are, and why you're here. Jesus Christ has carved out a place for you in His kingdom. He awaits with open arms, ready to lead you through every storm, celebrate every victory, and heal every wound. May you feel His presence and remember always: You Are His Child—and He loves you more than words can express.

Bibliography

Ballard, M. R. (2005). One more. In *Ensign*. The Church of Jesus Christ of Latter-day Saints.

Ballard, M. R. (2010). O that cunning plan of the evil one. In *Ensign*. The Church of Jesus Christ of Latter-day Saints.

Bednar, D. A. (2009). More diligent and concerned at home. In *Ensign*. The Church of Jesus Christ of Latter-day Saints.

Bednar, D. A. (2011). Patterns of light: Discerning truth. Deseret Book.

Callister, T. R. (2011). The infinite atonement. Deseret Book.

Christofferson, D. T. (2010). Reflections on a consecrated life. In *Ensign*. The Church of Jesus Christ of Latter-day Saints.

Christofferson, D. T. (2015). Why marriage, why family. In *Ensign*. The Church of Jesus Christ of Latter-day Saints.

Doctrine and Covenants 58:26–28; 88:6; (n.d.). The Church of Jesus Christ of Latter-day Saints (2013).

Eyring, H. B. (1999). Finding safety in counsel. In *Ensign*. The Church of Jesus Christ of Latter-day Saints.

Eyring, H. B. (2002). A testimony of Jesus Christ. In *Ensign*. The Church of Jesus Christ of Latter-day Saints.

Eyring, H. B. (2007). O remember, remember. In *Ensign*. The Church of Jesus Christ of Latter-day Saints.

Hafen, B. C. (1992). The atonement: All for all. In *Ensign*. The Church of Jesus Christ of Latter-day Saints.

Hales, R. D. (1998). The eternal family. In *Ensign*. The Church of Jesus Christ of Latter-day Saints.

Holland, J. R. (1999). An high priest of good things to come. In *Ensign*. The Church of Jesus Christ of Latter-day Saints.

Holland, J. R. (2002). A prayer for the children. In *Ensign*. The Church of Jesus Christ of Latter-day Saints.

Holland, J. R. (2006). Broken things to mend. In *Ensign*. The Church of Jesus Christ of Latter-day Saints.

Holland, J. R. (2012). The laborers in the vineyard [Conference address]. The Church of Jesus Christ of Latter-day Saints.

Holland, J. R. (2013). Like a broken vessel. In *Ensign*. The Church of Jesus Christ of Latter-day Saints.

Holland, J. R. (2014). Are we not all beggars? In *Ensign*. The Church of Jesus Christ of Latter-day Saints.

John 8:12; 10:10; 11:3; 15:15; 16:33; 24:13–32; 1 Samuel 1:9–20; 1 Kings 19:12; Acts 2:42; 2 Corinthians 1:4; 1 Thessalonians 4:13; 1 Kings 19:12; Romans 8:16–17; Luke 10:34–35; 22:44; 23:34; 24:32; Matthew 5:14–16; 5:39; 5:44; 11:28; 22:37–39; 23:37; 26:38–40; 26:39–44; 27:46; John 3:16; 8:12; 10:10; 13:4–17; 14:18; 15:15; 16:25; 16:33; 19:20; Revelation 21:4; 1 Corinthians 12:12–27; 1 Thessalonians 4:13 (n.d.). *The Holy Bible, King James Version*. The Church of Jesus Christ of Latter-day Saints.

King, M. L. Jr. (1963). Strength to love. Fortress Press.

Maxwell, N. A. (1974). Why not now?. Deseret Book.

Maxwell, N. A. (1977). All these things shall give thee experience. In *Ensign*. The Church of Jesus Christ of Latter-day Saints.

Maxwell, N. A. (1978). Notwithstanding my weakness. Deseret Book.

Maxwell, N. A. (1979). Deposition of a disciple. Deseret Book.

Maxwell, N. A. (1985). Notwithstanding my weakness. Deseret Book.

Maxwell, N. A. (1990). The stern but sweet seventh commandment. Bookcraft.

Maxwell, N. A. (1991). Encircled in the arms of His love. In *Ensign*. The Church of Jesus Christ of Latter-day Saints.

McConkie, B. R. (1972). The Purifying Power of Gethsemane. In *Ensign*. The Church of Jesus Christ of Latter-day Saints.

Monson, T. S. (2008). Finding joy in the journey. In *Ensign*. The Church of Jesus Christ of Latter-day Saints.

Monson, T. S. (2010). Be of good cheer. In *Ensign*. The Church of Jesus Christ of Latter-day Saints.

Mosiah 27; 28:4; (n.d.). *The Book of Mormon: Another Testament of Jesus Christ*. The Church of Jesus Christ of Latter-day Saints.

Nelson, R. M. (1990). Lessons from Eve. In *Ensign*. The Church of Jesus Christ of Latter-day Saints.

Nelson, R. M. (1995). Perfection pending. In *Ensign*. The Church of Jesus Christ of Latter-day Saints.

Nelson, R. M. (2016). Joy and spiritual survival. In *Ensign*. The Church of Jesus Christ of Latter-day Saints.

Nelson, R. M. (2017). Drawing the power of Jesus Christ into our lives. In *Ensign*. The Church of Jesus Christ of Latter-day Saints.

Nelson, R. M. (2018). Revelation for the church, revelation for our lives. In *Ensign*. The Church of Jesus Christ of Latter-day Saints.

Nelson, R. M. (2019). The covenant path. In *Ensign*. The Church of Jesus Christ of Latter-day Saints.

Nelson, R. M. (2020). Embrace the future with faith. In *Ensign*. The Church of Jesus Christ of Latter-day Saints.

Orson F. Whitney. (1921). *Through the gateway of sorrow to the mount of vision*. Deseret Book.

Packer, B. K. (1977). Teach ye diligently. Deseret Book.

Packer, B. K. (1983). Personal revelation: The gift, the test, and the promise. In *Ensign*. The Church of Jesus Christ of Latter-day Saints.

Rasband, R. A. (2016). Lest thou forget. In *Ensign*. The Church of Jesus Christ of Latter-day Saints.

Rasband, R. A. (2017). By divine design. In *Ensign*. The Church of Jesus Christ of Latter-day Saints.

Renlund, D. G. (2015). Latter-day saints keep on trying. In *Ensign*. The Church of Jesus Christ of Latter-day Saints.

Romans 8:16–17. (n.d.). *The Holy Bible, King James Version*. The Church of Jesus Christ of Latter-day Saints.

Scott, R. G. (2009). To acquire spiritual guidance. In *Ensign*. The Church of Jesus Christ of Latter-day Saints.

Smith, J. (1842). *History of the Church*, vol. 4. Deseret Book.

Stevenson, G. E. (2017). Your divine nature and eternal destiny. In *Ensign*. The Church of Jesus Christ of Latter-day Saints.

The Book of Mormon: Another Testament of Jesus Christ. (n.d.). The Church of Jesus Christ of Latter-day Saints.

The Church of Jesus Christ of Latter-day Saints. (n.d.). Joseph Smith—History. In *Pearl of Great Price*.

Uchtdorf, D. F. (2007). Point of safe return. In *Ensign*. The Church of Jesus Christ of Latter-day Saints.

Uchtdorf, D. F. (2008). The infinite power of hope. In *Ensign*. The Church of Jesus Christ of Latter-day Saints.

Uchtdorf, D. F. (2009). The love of God. In *Ensign*. The Church of Jesus Christ of Latter-day Saints.

Uchtdorf, D. F. (2010). You matter to him. In *Ensign*. The Church of Jesus Christ of Latter-day Saints.

Uchtdorf, D. F. (2012). The why of priesthood service. In *Ensign*. The Church of Jesus Christ of Latter-day Saints.

Uchtdorf, D. F. (2014). Receiving a testimony of light and truth. In *Ensign*. The Church of Jesus Christ of Latter-day Saints.

Uchtdorf, D. F. (2017). A yearning for home. In *Ensign*. The Church of Jesus Christ of Latter-day Saints.

Wirthlin, J. B. (2008). Come what may, and love it. In *Ensign*. The Church of Jesus Christ of Latter-day Saints.

If you would like to learn more about Jesus Christ and His infinite love and grace, please scan the QR code below, or call:

888-537-7700

Made in the USA
Las Vegas, NV
06 May 2025